P 14, 5, 40, 127

D-25.

D1616234

NUTRITION, FOOD, AND MAN

An Interdisciplinary Perspective

NUTRITION, FOOD, AND MAN

An Interdisciplinary Perspective

Paul B. Pearson and
J. Richard Greenwell, Editors

THE UNIVERSITY OF ARIZONA PRESS
Tucson, Arizona

About the Editors . . .

Paul B. Pearson is former Director of the Biology Program of the U.S. Atomic Energy Commission (1949-1958), Senior Staff Member of the Ford Foundation (1958-1963), President of the Nutrition Foundation (1963-1972), and has been on the faculty and administration of numerous universities. The author of many publications, Dr. Pearson joined the University of Arizona faculty in 1974 as a Professor of Nutrition.

J. Richard Greenwell spent six years in Peru, and joined the University of Arizona arid lands program in 1974. With training in anthropology and psychology, his main interests relate to multidisciplinary approaches to scientific problem-solving and the public understanding of science. Since 1978 he has been Secretary, Arid Lands Natural Resources Committee, and Coordinator, Office of International Agricultural Programs.

The University of Arizona Press
Copyright ©1980
The Arizona Board of Regents
All Rights Reserved
Manufactured in the U.S.A.

Library of Congress Cataloging in Publication Data
Main entry under title:
Nutrition, food, and man.

Based on papers which originated in an interdisciplinary seminar series on nutrition held at the University of Arizona in the fall of 1977.
1. Nutrition—Addresses, essays, lectures.
2. Malnutrition—Addresses, essays, lectures.
3. Food supply—Addresses, essays, lectures.
I. Pearson, Paul B., 1905-
II. Greenwell, J. Richard
TX355.5.N87   362.1'963905   80-10297

ISBN 0-8165-0691-4 (cloth)
ISBN 0-8165-0706-6 (paper)

The seminar series on which this publication is based was made possible by grant AID/TA-G1111 to The University of Arizona from the Office of Science and Technology, Development Support Bureau, U.S. Agency for International Development.

About the Authors

GEORG BORGSTROM, Ph.D., has been a member of the Science Board of the International Union of Nutritional Sciences (1956-62), a member of the Board of Trustees of the Population Reference Bureau in Washington, D.C. (1969-74), and has been the recipient of numerous honors and awards. He has authored many publications on the topics of nutritional aspects of food processing, protein utilization, world food issues, and food, water and energy relationships. Formerly head of the Swedish Institute of Food Preservation Research (1948-56), he joined the faculty of Michigan State University as a professor of food science and human nutrition in 1956.

JOSEPH G. BRAND, Ph.D., is active in research into sensory biophysics and the effect of food flavor on physiological regulation. He has served as a consultant to the Diet, Nutrition, and Cancer Program for the National Cancer Institute. In 1971 he became associated with the Monell Chemical Senses Center at the University of Pennsylvania.

DORIS H. CALLOWAY, Ph.D., has been a consultant to the National Academy of Sciences/National Research Council, the National Institutes of Health, the U.N.'s Food and Agriculture Organization, and the World Health Organization. She has served in an editorial capacity for a number of nutrition and scientific publications, and has written widely in the areas of human nutrition, protein-calorie requirements, and gastrointestinal studies. Dr. Calloway's academic positions have included service as Chairman of Food Science and Nutrition at Stanford Research Institute and head of the Department of Nutritional Sciences at the University of California, Berkeley.

JOAQUIN CRAVIOTO, M.D., is an internationally recognized authority on the diagnosis and prevention of infantile malnutrition and on the long and short-term effects of severe malnutrition on mental development, learning, and behavior. He is a member of the Protein Advisory Group of the United Nations and was Chairman of that group between 1973 and 1976. He has been Nutrition Officer in FAO's Latin American Area; Associate Director of the Institute of Nutrition of Central America and Panama, Pan American

Health Organization; President of the Mexican Society for Pediatric Research; Professor of Pediatrics at the National Autonomous University of Mexico; and Scientific Director of the National Institute of Child Health Sciences, Mexico City.

STANLEY N. GERSHOFF, Ph.D., has been a consultant to such national and international bodies as the U.S. Army Environmental Medicine Laboratories, the National Academy of Sciences/National Research Council, U.S. Departments of State and Agriculture (for Pakistan), UNICEF, the U.S. Senate Select Committee on Nutrition and Human Needs, and the Federal Trade Commission. A faculty member in nutrition at the Howard School of Public Health from 1952 to 1977, he has written over 100 research papers on nutritional biochemistry and physiology. Dr. Gershoff joined Tufts University in 1977 as a Professor of Nutrition and Director of the Tufts Nutrition Institute.

GAIL G. HARRISON, Ph.D., has been a participant at the Western Assembly on Population and Hunger (1975), a member of the World Food and Nutrition Study of the National Academy of Sciences/National Research Council (1976), a consultant to the Harvard/AID Cereal Fortification Project (1976), a member of the Executive Board of the Committee on Nutritional Anthropology of the Society for Medical Anthropology, and an Associate Editor of the *Journal of Nutrition Education*. She is the co-author of two books and has authored many published papers in the areas of human nutrition, epidemiology of nutritional diseases, and medical anthropology. In 1976 she joined the faculty of the University of Arizona's Departments of Family and Community Medicine, Pediatrics, and Nutrition and Food Science.

DERRICK B. JELLIFFE, M.D., has been a consultant on at least 45 occasions to governments in Africa, Asia, and Latin America, and to international organizations such as WHO, UNICEF, and PAHO. He has participated in professional meetings in 31 different countries, mainly in such areas as protein-calorie malnutrition of children, nutrition education, pediatrics, and breast feeding, and has authored some 300 books and papers. In 1971 Dr. Jelliffe became Head of the Division of Population, Family, and International Health at UCLA's School of Public Health and professor of pediatrics in the UCLA School of Medicine.

E. F. PATRICE JELLIFFE, M.P.H., has taught nurses in countries throughout the world, including Iraq, India, Nigeria, and the West Indies. Her research into public health, nutrition, and child health has been under the auspices of such agencies as the International Child Health Surveys, WHO, and the Caribbean Food and Nutrition Institute, and her service to governmental agencies has included work with AID, UNICEF, the Pan American Health Organization, and the UN Protein Advisory Group. In 1975 she joined the faculty of the Division of Population, Family, and International Health of the School of Public Health, UCLA.

MORLEY R. KARE, Ph.D., has been a professor of physiology at Cornell University, North Carolina State University, and the University of Pennsylvania, where he is also the director of the Monell Chemical Senses Center. He has served on many national and international commissions and committees, including the Executive Committee of the Nutrition Foundation's Board of Trustees, and he was general chairman at the 1976 International Conference on the Chemical Senses and Nutrition. He is the author of over 150 scientific publications related to his principle research interest, the comparative physiology of taste.

GLENN LIPPMAN, M.D., graduated from the University of Arizona College of Medicine in 1979, receiving awards for excellence in both Obstetrics and Psychiatry, and joined the house staff at the Arizona Health Sciences Center, specializing in Obstetrics. His research includes federally supported work in the field of iron nutrition in newborns, as well as ongoing investigation into the effects of nutrition on immune response.

MAX MILNER, Ph.D., has been a Senior Food Technologist with UNICEF (1959-71), the Scientific Secretary and Director of the Secretariat, Protein-Calorie Advisory Group of the United Nations System (1971-75), and Coordinator of the NSF/MIT Protein Resources Study (1975-76). He has also been a consultant to FAO, to AID's Technical Assistance Bureau, and to the Office of Technology Assessment of the Congress. He was official delegate to the UN's World Food Conference in Rome in 1974. In 1976 Dr. Milner became Associate Director of the International Nutrition Policy and Planning Program at the Massachusetts Institute of Technology, and in September of 1978 joined the staff of the American Institute of Nutrition in Bethesda, Maryland as Executive Officer.

MIRIAM MUNOZ de CHAVEZ, M.S., was Director of the Department of Nutritional Education in Mexico's National Nutrition Institute between 1964 and 1977. She is a member of such international bodies as the International Union of Nutritional Societies, the Pan American Health Organization (Committee on Nutritional Education), and the U.S. National Academy of Sciences (Committee on Nutritional Surveys), and has written numerous articles in Mexican and international nutritional and public health journals. She is the Coordinator of Mexico's National Food and Nutrition Program.

MICHAEL NAIM, Ph.D., was a Research Associate and later Associate Member at the Monell Chemical Senses Center of the University of Pennsylvania between 1974 and 1977. His research into the biochemistry and physiology of the chemical senses has been especially focused on the effect of food flavors on food utilization. In 1977 he became a Research Associate at the Hebrew University Medical School and in 1978 joined the Faculty of Agriculture at the Hebrew University in Rehovot, Israel.

PAUL B. PEARSON, Ph.D., became part-time head of the Department of Nutrition at the National Autonomous University in Guadalajara, Mexico, in 1973, and joined the faculty of the University of Arizona in 1974 after a long career with such institutions as Johns Hopkins, the U.S. Atomic Energy Commission, and the Ford Foundation. He served as the President and Scientific Director of the Nutrition Foundation (1963-72), and has served on many national committees under the auspices of the National Research Council, the Department of Agriculture, and the Executive Office of the President. He is the author of over 140 scientific publications in such areas as amino acid mineral metabolism, effects of various nutrients on embryonic development, and the effects of nutrition on socioeconomic development.

NEVIN S. SCRIMSHAW, M.D., Ph.D., has served as researcher and advisor with such bodies as the National Institutes of Health; the Commission on International Relations, President's Food and Nutrition Study (NAS); NAS Task Force on Food/Health/Population; WHO; and the Protein Calorie Advisory Group of the United Nations. He became a Senior Advisor to the UN World Hunger Programme in 1975. He is the author of over 400 scientific articles on various aspects of human and animal nutrition, nutrition and infection, agricultural and food chemistry, and public health. In 1961 he became Head of the Department of Nutrition and Food Science at the Massachusetts Institute of Technology.

OTTO F. SIEBER, M.D., directed the Section on Infectious Disease and the Virology/Immunology Research Laboratory at the University of Arizona Health Sciences Center between 1976 and 1979. He has also been associated with such institutions as the University of Colorado Medical Center; Haile Salassie I University in Addis Ababa, Ethiopia; the U.S. Army Medical Research and Nutrition Laboratory, Denver; and the American Academy of Pediatrics, New Orleans. He has published widely in the areas of immunology, infectious diseases, nutrition, pediatrics, and medical education. In 1979 he became Professor of Pediatrics, Director of Education and Associate Chairman, Texas Tech School of Medicine and Regional Academic Health Center, El Paso, Texas.

WILLIAM A. STINI, Ph.D., joined the University of Arizona's faculty in 1976 as a professor of anthropology after teaching at Cornell University and the University of Kansas. He has published and lectured widely on human nutrition, human adaptability, and the relationship of diets and cancer, and he has been a consultant to the National Cancer Institute, the National Institutes of Health, and the National Science Foundation. Dr. Stini undertook an anthropometric and serological study of kwashiorkor-affected populations in Colombia in 1967 and 1968.

D.I.C. WANG, Ph.D., has been a consultant to a number of commissions and agencies on food production and alternative protein sources, including the Committee for US/USSR Technology Exchange (regarding single-cell protein production) and a committee of the National Academy of Sciences on alternative energy sources for developing countries. He has lectured at the University of Osaka under the auspices of UNICEF. He is the author of over 100 articles and a Professor of Biochemical Engineering in the Department of Nutrition and Food Science, Massachusetts Institute of Technology.

Contents

Foreword

Human beings suffer from several kinds of malnutrition. They can be harmed by eating too little food, or too much food, or by the wrong amounts or balance of particular elements in their diets. These types of malnutrition are found in all countries; undernourishment is particularly widespread in the developing countries, while other kinds of malnutrition involving obesity and related problems are prominent in the more affluent industrialized countries. Contributing to the extent of malnutrition is the absence or weakness of policies and programs to foster the best use of available food supplies; this is true on both a national and institutional basis. In developing and developed countries alike, governments, institutions, private organizations, food producers, advertisers, and individuals continually make decisions that affect nutritional status on the basis of less than adequate knowledge of nutritional consequences.

Nutrition, Food, and Man has been prepared by a group of outstanding authorities in the field of nutrition to examine a number of questions currently in the forefront of research into nutrition, malnutrition, and the problems of food distribution in the world of the late twentieth century. The volume begins with an introductory survey by co-editor Paul B. Pearson, an old friend and former President of the Nutrition Foundation, which reviews the world food situation, indicates the relationships between malnutrition and disease, and outlines future prospects.

In the developing countries malnutrition causes millions of premature deaths each year. In some societies, 40 percent of children die before they reach the age of five, mostly from nutrition-related causes. A substantial proportion of the survivors suffer handicaps of learning, behavior, and work capacity because of inadequate diets and recurring illness. Derrick B. Jelliffe and E.F. Patrice Jelliffe address the cultural, biological, and programmatic considerations of infant nutrition in developing countries, with special emphasis on the importance of breast feeding as opposed to artificial feeding. Drs. Otto Sieber and Glenn Lippman have contributed a chapter on the relationships between nutritional status and resistance to infectious diseases. Miriam Muñoz de Chavez discusses the severe socioeconomic problems brought about by malnutrition in developing countries, using Mexican studies of physical and mental development as her focus. Ms. Chavez, who was Director of the Department of Nutritional Education in Mexico's National Nutrition Institute between 1964 and 1977, also analyzes national nutrition policies in Mexico. The results of longitudinal studies of the lasting effects of malnutrition on children's neurological development and learning are discussed by another Mexican authority, Joaquin Cravioto, M.D., Scientific Director of the National Institute of Child Health Sciences in Mexico City.

Since the 1920's, the questions of what nutrients are required by man and in what amounts have been largely answered. Research today in agriculture, nutrition, public health, and other disciplines, is attempting to meet the challenge of world nutrition needs in a variety of ways, including the development of new food substances and new methods of enriching diets. William Stini's chapter on "Human Adaptability to Nutritional Stress" takes an evolutionary approach in discussing the wide variety of foods humans eat, the limits of nutritional stress tolerance, and the question of adult starvation. Programs to fortify various foods by enrichment with supplements are examined by Stanley N. Gershoff, who shows how little is really known about the effectiveness of such attempts. The outlook for new protein resources by Drs. Milner, Scrimshaw, and Wang examines the research being done in developing a wide variety of new kinds of food to supply protein to the world. Factors which may affect the acceptability of these new proteins – the relationship between taste and food preferences, food quality, food digestion, and the modification of basic tastes – are discussed in the chapter by Joseph Brand, Morley Kare, and Michael Naim.

Although nutritional requirements need to be determined more precisely and the classification and evaluation of new essential nutrients and nutrient sources must be continued, it is clear that the major and much more complex problems we now face are economic, political, behavioral, environmental, and educational. The development of national and world food and nutrition policies is a complex but vital process. Georg Borgstrom is critical of existing policies and measures in his examination of the disparity between the rapidly expanding world population and future potential food resources. Doris Calloway discusses the development and accuracy of the current standards for human protein requirements, the controversy regarding the existence of a "protein gap" or a "calorie gap" between nations, and the setting of priorities. The final chapter by Gail Harrison appropriately addresses the nutrition policies which governments should adopt in attempting to forestall or alleviate future food crises.

I recommend this volume highly for its intensely interesting and perceptive treatment of the complex array of problems the world faces in delivering adequate, nutritious food to every person, every day.

Herbert E. Carter
Head, Department of Biochemistry
The University of Arizona

Former Chairman, National Science Board
National Science Foundation, Washington, D.C.

Editors' Note

Interest in nutrition has increased enormously since the 1950s, both at the popular level and at the research level. We believe this book will help to bridge the gap between the latest research findings on the topic and the public understanding of the nutritional sciences. We have been very fortunate in bringing together the writings of some of the most distinguished research leaders and educators in nutrition into one volume, a volume which we believe will be useful to the public, to students, and to professionals and paraprofessionals for many years to come.

The seeds of this volume originated in an Interdisciplinary Seminar Series on Nutrition held at the University of Arizona in the fall of 1977. The papers from that seminar series have been greatly edited, and in some cases expanded, to produce a well-rounded, comprehensive volume on the state of the art in nutrition. We thank all the authors for their efforts and for their patience.

We would also like to thank all those at the University of Arizona who have assisted and supported us in the preparation of this volume. Our particular thanks go to Biochemistry Department Head Herbert E. Carter, who has been our guiding light since the volume's inception, to Jack D. Johnson, Director of the Office of Arid Lands Studies, and to W. Gerald Matlock, Director of International Agricultural Programs, for striving hard to make this volume a reality. Thanks are also due to A. Richard Kassander, Vice President for Research, for financial support, and to Mary Gretchen Limper, who provided invaluable editorial assistance.

We would also like to express our appreciation to The University of Arizona Press, in particular to Elizabeth Shaw, Assistant Director and Editorial Coordinator, and Marshall Townsend, Director, for advice and assistance beyond the call of duty as publishers.

Paul B. Pearson
J. Richard Greenwell

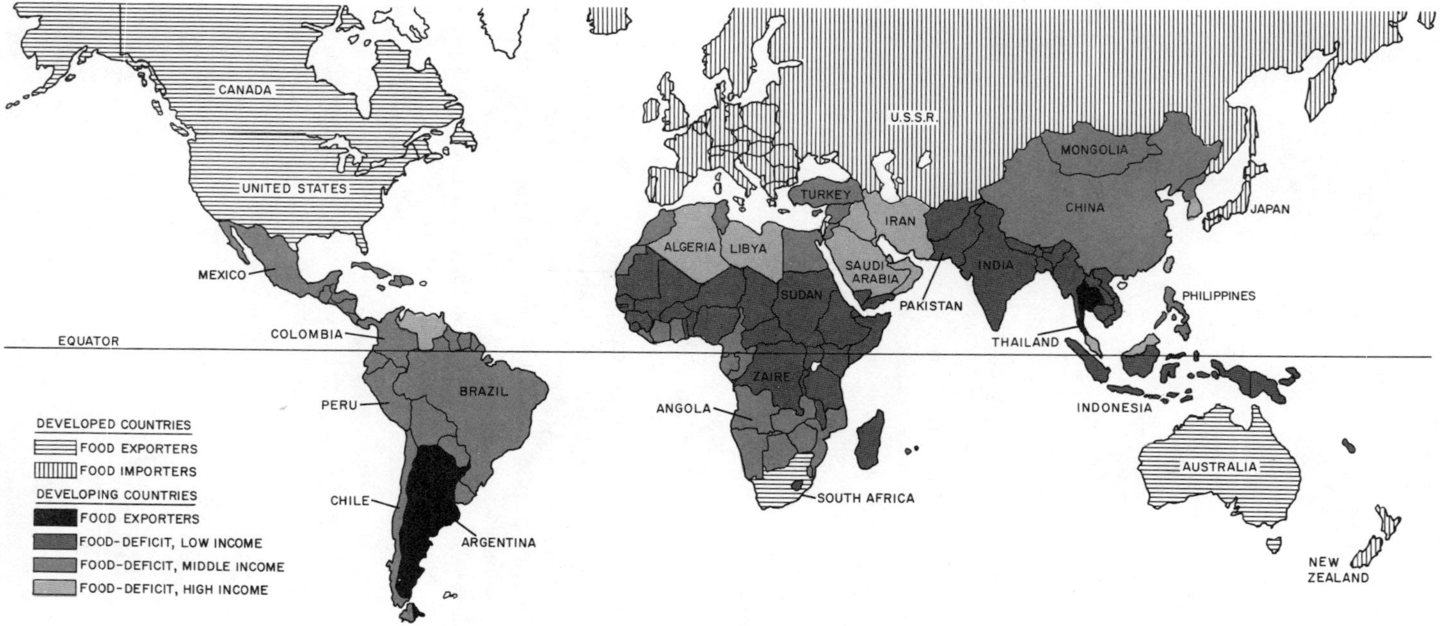
CANADA
UNITED STATES
MEXICO
COLOMBIA
PERU
BRAZIL
CHILE
ARGENTINA
EQUATOR
U.S.S.R.
MONGOLIA
CHINA
JAPAN
TURKEY
IRAN
ALGERIA
LIBYA
SAUDI ARABIA
SUDAN
PAKISTAN
INDIA
PHILIPPINES
THAILAND
ZAIRE
ANGOLA
INDONESIA
AUSTRALIA
SOUTH AFRICA
NEW ZEALAND
DEVELOPED COUNTRIES
FOOD EXPORTERS
FOOD IMPORTERS
DEVELOPING COUNTRIES
FOOD EXPORTERS
FOOD-DEFICIT, LOW INCOME
FOOD-DEFICIT, MIDDLE INCOME
FOOD-DEFICIT, HIGH INCOME

Fig. 1.1

World Nutrition: An Overview

Paul B. Pearson

The "world food crisis" became headline news in the 1970's and the concern of governments in countries throughout the world. The global demand for food often exceeded available supplies, while reserves were reduced to a dangerously low level. Food prices rose as never before. Disruptions in food supplies and commercial markets fueled public anxiety and concern. Nutrition is one of the main determinants of health, now recognized as one of the rights of mankind. The problem of malnutrition is comprised of numerous components (Eckholm and Record, 1976), some only recognized within the 1970's, some known for centuries, but all interrelated.

Malnutrition afflicts a far larger proportion of mankind than any other malady or disease. It is a chronic condition which seems to be getting more prevalent rather than declining in many areas of the world. Long term corrective and preventive actions and contributions from many disciplines will be required in meeting this problem. These actions must necessarily involve a variety of areas, including agricultural practices and economic and social policies.

The fundamental responsibility of any society should be to insure the well-being of all of its members, including the insurance of the right to adequate nutrition. The presence of malnutrition in any country or society, then, reflects the failure of that society to meet the fundamental needs of its people. Virtually no country has fully met the needs. Malnutrition, in one form or another, exists in varying degrees in practically every affluent, industrialized, and developing country in the world.

The magnitude of the problem becomes more obvious when one considers that, according to the International Food Policy Research Institute (IFPRI) (Gavan, 1977), 1.2 to 1.3 billion people were characterized as undernourished in 1975. Most of these were in low-income Asian and sub-Saharan countries, where 70 percent of the population is considered undernourished. It is very likely that half of the people alive in the 1970's at some time in their lives went through a period of inadequate nutrition.

The primary geographic areas of malnutrition include Central America, most of tropical South America, most of Africa, much of the Near East, and the southern portion of mainland Asia. It is significant that the high prevalence of malnutrition tends to be concentrated in the tropical or semi-tropical regions of the world. A look at figure 1.1 shows, as would be

expected, that the food deficit regions in the world (Wortman, 1976) cover
essentially the same areas as do the regions of malnutrition. These are also the
low-income regions of the world.

Infants, children, and pregnant and lactating women are most vulnerable
to the adverse effects of malnutrition; these groups tend to have higher
requirements for many essential nutrients. At the same time, many of them
are the ones least able to provide for their own needs. As indicated in figure
1.2, infant and child mortality run high in those countries with food deficits
and are highly correlated with low per capita income and with illiteracy. The
rate of mortality in children from birth to one year in the developing
countries may be 20 to 40 times that in the developed countries (Bouvier and
van der Tak, 1976).

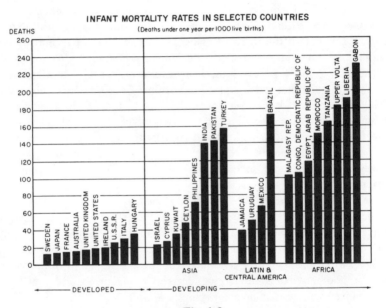

Fig. 1.2

In many of the developing countries, the poorest 20 percent of the
population has only half the per capita calorie intake of the top 10 percent.
Low-income groups invariably consist of a high proportion of uneducated
people of relatively low social status. Many of their children die at an early
age from disease and malnutrition. The surviving children suffer from chronic
malnutrition, internal parasites, recurrent bouts of diarrhea, and infectious
diseases. Both their physical growth and mental development are impaired.
Consequently, their capacity for learning and achieving an education is
limited. Their work performance or earning capacity as they grow to maturity
is further reduced by continued inadequate nutrition. They become parents

at an early age, and their children are almost inevitably destined to follow the same vicious cycle. On the other hand, the affluent sections of the population tend to have well-nourished and healthy children who are able to take advantage of the superior educational opportunities they are afforded.

In the developing countries, highest priority should be given to alleviating protein-calorie malnutrition, anemias, xerophthalmia, and endemic goiter. These common nutritional maladies affect a large proportion of the population in these countries.

Nutritionally, the most precarious period in the life of the child is the period of transition from breast feeding to a diet of semi-solid and solid foods. In this period, children are likely to have diets that do not provide adequate protein, and the protein coming primarily or entirely from cereals and other plant foods will be low in one or more essential amino acids. This is at a time when the fast-growing child has exceptionally high protein requirements. The foods that are available are usually high in carbohydrates and low in protein because these are the least expensive.

The increasing tendency in developing countries for mothers not to breast feed their infants is a major factor contributing to the high mortality of infants during the first year of life. Improved economic conditions discourage breast feeding. There are more opportunities for the mothers to work, leaving the infant at home to be cared for by an older sister, grandmother, or other relative. Inevitably, this means bottle feeding, with a greatly increased risk for the infant. Chile, which had an infant death rate of 123 per 1000 live births in the late 1960's, is representative of this situation. This rate was much higher than it was two or three decades previously, when there was far less opportunity for the mother to be employed away from home. In many cases, the family cannot afford to purchase adequate amounts of formula foods, which may require 30 to 50 percent of their cash income, and because of ignorance and lack of facilities, the formula food will be reconstituted with contaminated water and in unsterilized bottles. Without refrigeration, this provides an ideal medium for the growth of micro-organisms, which can be the cause of severe, recurring, and often fatal diarrhea.

The Inter-American Investigation of Mortality in Childhood (Puffer and Serrano, 1973) found that eight percent of deaths in children six months to two years of age had malnutrition as the underlying or main causes and 41 percent had it as an associated cause.

Xerophthalmia, caused by a deficiency of vitamin A, affects the eyes, impairing vision, and ultimately results in blindness. It is prevalent in regions with long, dry seasons during which there is likely to be a scarcity of common sources of provitamin A, namely, green leafy and yellow vegetables and yellow fruit. In some major regions of the world xerophthalmia due to lack of vitamin A is so common that it is considered a serious public health problem. While vitamin A deficiency may become apparent at any age, it occurs most frequently after weaning and through the third and fourth years of life.

Anemia, due to an iron deficiency, is widespread, especially among pregnant and lactating women, and is found in children of all regions, including even the developed countries. In temperate zones, 20 to 30 percent of pregnant women may be anemic, and the frequency of anemia may be as much as 40 percent for infants in the first year of life. In tropical areas, parasitic infestations and the poor availability of dietary iron contribute to the high prevalence of anemia. Anemia reduces the oxygen-carrying capacity of the blood, thereby decreasing the supply of oxygen to the tissues, and in turn impairing work capacity.

Endemic goiter, due to a lack of iodine in the diet, has been reported from all continents. It occurs in all high mountain ranges: the Alps, the Andes, the Himalayas, the Rocky Mountains. This disease can be eliminated in a dramatic way by supplying minute quantities of iodine. The most feasible means of doing so is by adding iodine or iodates to ordinary table salt at the rate of 1 part to between 25,000 and 50,000 parts of salt.

The dramatic reduction of goiter in Colombia by the introduction of iodized salt in 1950 is shown in figure 1.3. This action was not taken until more than a hundred years after Boussingault, a noted French chemist, found that salt from the ocean was high in iodine, whereas salt from the mountain areas was low. On the basis of this observation, Boussingault recommended to the government of Colombia at the time that ocean salt be used rather than that from the salt mines in the Andes.

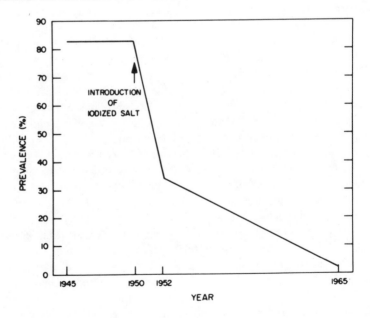

Fig. 1.3

The above-mentioned nutritional problems are, for the most part, the result of unavailability of the foods that provide adequate quantities of the nutrients essential for good health. This is not to imply that serious nutritional problems affecting the health of the individual do not occur in affluent countries with food surpluses as well.

In the developed countries, obesity is a serious public health problem. It is a reflection of an affluent society that consumes too much food with dietary patterns not necessarily conducive to good health over the life span. Obesity is associated with the risk of increased morbidity and mortality (Angel, 1974). All cardiovascular diseases together, including heart attacks, strokes, arterial diseases, and others, account for about one-half of adult deaths in developed countries. Ischemic heart disease accounts for one in every three deaths in the U.S., claiming annually some 700,000 lives. The World Health Organization (WHO) data for 18 Western countries reveal an increase of 50 percent in the incidence of coronary heart disease between 1950 and 1968 for persons aged 35 to 44 years. Since 1950, it has been recognized that signs of atherosclerosis may appear in teenagers as well as in the middle aged in the U.S. Thus, it appears that faulty diet at a fairly early age may be a contributing factor to cardiovascular disease in later life. Studies suggest that bottle fed babies are more prone to be obese and to develop into obese children than are babies that are breast fed.

Dental caries, which are definitely related to dietary patterns, are another widespread public health problem. They are more prevalent in developed countries than in some of the developing ones. The cariogenic nature of sucrose and other free sugars, in contrast to starch, has been known for some time. There is a high correlation between the amount of sucrose consumed and the incidence of dental caries. When the intake of sucrose is restricted, as occurred during World War II in Europe, there is a corresponding decrease in dental caries in children.

Evidence has also been accumulating that nutrition and dietary patterns are factors in the etiology of some types of cancer. In fact, during the 1970's this was one of the active areas of cancer research.

There are gross differences in the composition of diets of populations in the affluent developed countries and in the developing food deficit countries (Beaton and Bengoa, 1976). Low-income diets in all countries are characterized by a high proportion of carbohydrates, low fat, low animal protein, and low total protein of relatively low quality. In the developed countries, there has been, since 1950, an increase in the consumption of animal foods, associated with higher incomes. This trend is also occurring in the developing countries, and is already well established within the higher income segment of the population in these countries.

Average consumption of meats, including poultry, in the U.S., Australia, and Argentina leveled off in the 1970's at close to 250 pounds (carcass weight) annually per capita. In contrast, Japan's per capita intake of 44 pounds, exclusive of fish, in 1974 was an increase of more than 425 percent over its 1961 intake, while the average meat consumption in many developing countries was below 20 pounds annually.

In the developing countries, cereals and tubers provide the main constituents of the diet, and are consumed directly. In the U.S. and Canada, over 900 of the 1000 kilograms of cereals available per person, or 90 percent, is used for animal production, with the percentages only slightly lower for such countries as France and Germany. In contrast, in China, of each 250 kilograms of cereal available per person, 160 are used directly as bread, rice, or other grain-based foods. The trend toward higher conversion of grain to animal products is likely to be extended as countries improve their economic status, thus putting additional pressure on food supply.

Farm animals utilizing plant proteins formulated into balanced rations are relatively inefficient in converting plant proteins into animal proteins. Estimates indicate that one acre of productive land will provide man's protein needs for only 77 days in the form of beef, as milk 236 days, as rice 654 days, as corn meal 773 days, and as soybean protein as much as 2224 days. Poultry, in the form of eggs, is the most efficient converter of plant protein and energy to edible animal forms of these nutrients (26 percent), whereas beef cattle and sheep convert less than 4 percent to animal protein and energy (Janick, Noller, and Rhykerd, 1976). However, since cattle and sheep can consume roughage and forages that are not edible to man, they are not competing with humans for plant proteins until the animals are moved into the feed lot.

In general, there is a high correlation between the rate of population increase, the per capita GNP, and the extent of malnutrition in a society (World Population Data Sheet, 1978). Countries with the highest infant and child mortality have high birth rates and low per capita GNP. The crux of the problem is a rapidly increasing population in most developing countries, due partly to the success of programs to eliminate communicable diseases, without equal increases in food availability. The birth rate in the less developed countries, where malnutrition is prevalent, has remained high (table 1.1), while the death rate has decreased and life expectancy increased. Consequently, there has been a rapid increase in the rate of growth of the population in these countries.

Robert S. McNamara, President of the World Bank, speaking at the Massachusetts Institute of Technology in 1977, stated: "Short of nuclear war itself, population growth is the greatest issue the world faces over the decades immediately ahead. Indeed, in many ways, rampant population growth is an even more dangerous and subtle threat to the world than thermonuclear war, for it is intrinsically less subject to rational safeguards, and less amenable to organized control" (McNamara, 1977). The population growth of the planet

Table 1.1
POPULATION GROWTH and GROSS NATIONAL PRODUCT

Country	Rate of Annual Population Growth (%)	Years to Double	GNP Per Capita (U.S. $)
Egypt	2.5	41	280
Ghana	2.9	24	580
Liberia	2.9	24	610
Niger	2.7	26	340
Kenya	3.3	21	240
Uganda	3.0	23	240
Cameroon	2.0	35	290
Iraq	3.4	20	1,390
Israel	2.1	33	3,920
Turkey	2.3	30	990
Bangladesh	2.7	26	110
Pakistan	3.0	23	170
Philippines	2.5	28	410
Japan	1.0	69	4,910
China	1.4	50	410
U.S.	0.6	116	7,510
Canada	0.9	77	7,890
Mexico	3.4	20	1,090
Cuba	1.5	46	860
Dominican Republic	3.0	23	780
Argentina	1.3	53	1,550
Colombia	2.4	29	630
Denmark	0.2	347	7,450
Ireland	1.1	63	2,560
Sweden	0.1	693	8,670
United Kingdom	0.0	–	4,020

(Data from 1978 World Population Data Sheet of the Population Reference Bureau, Inc.)

is not under the exclusive control of a few governments, but rather in the hands of literally hundreds of millions of individual parents who will ultimately determine the outcome. The population problem is the central determinant of mankind's future. For the first 99 percent of man's existence, population grew very slowly. For the last one percent of his history it has grown in a great rush. It took mankind more than a million years to reach a world population of one billion. At the annual growth rate recorded in the 1970's of about two percent per year, the fifth billion could be added by 1990.

The key to the future of mankind is the extent to which we succeed in bringing into balance food production and population. Means of increasing world food production and production per unit of land are available with striking demonstrations of success. The ability of China to produce enough food for its more than 800 million people on 11 percent of its total available land is an impressive example. It should be noted that the land mass of China exceeds that of the U.S., including Alaska and Hawaii, by only about 25 percent. Malnutrition was rife in China in 1930, but it had been practically eliminated, even though the per capita income was still relatively low, by the end of the 1970's.

The factors affecting reduction of human fertility are extremely complex. It appears likely that there are a number of key linkages between fertility reduction and certain specific elements of socio-economic development. The factors that appear to be the most important are health, education, broadly distributed economic growth, urbanization, and the enhanced status of women. While these factors are at work in varying degrees in the developing world, their effect is too slow to meet the impending food-population dilemma.

Food production from 1960 to 1975 increased in both the developed and the developing countries at similar rates. It does not follow that the nutritional status of peoples in the developing areas improved significantly (Wortman, 1976). This increased food production was largely nullified by the rapid population growth, resulting in virtually no per capita increase in food availability. The projected future food deficit in terms of cereals, as calculated by the International Food Policy Research Institute, is shown in figure 1.4.

If the people of the developing countries are to be fed, the food will have to come from their own soil. The surplus food production of a few exporting countries cannot be counted on over a long period. Furthermore, even over shorter periods, the developing countries do not have funds for the importation of food year after year. Most of the developing countries are better endowed for agricultural development than for any other kind of economic advance, and could significantly increase food yields per acre, and also could extend the area of cultivated land to the extent of satisfying the food needs of their population (Hopper, 1976). The challenge before the developed countries is to assist the developing countries in utilizing and modernizing their resources so as to bring into balance food production and population.

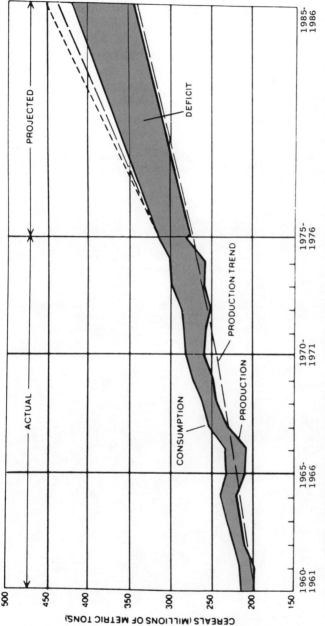

FUTURE FOOD DEFICIT in the developing countries is foreseen. Actual data are given, for cereal production and consumption in the market-economy developing nations that have food deficits, up to 1975–1976. The trend of production since 1960–1961 was calculated and the trend line projected to 1985–1986. Future demand was projected from current human consumption on the basis of population growth and alternative assumptions about growth of per capita income.

Fig. 1.4

10 PAUL B. PEARSON

References

Angel, A.
1974 Physiology of obesity. *Canadian Medical Association Journal 110:*540.

Beaton, G.H., and J.M. Bengoa
1976 Nutrition in Preventive Medicine. *World Health Organization Monograph No. 62,* Geneva, p. 482.

Bouvier, L.F., and J. van der Tak
1976 Infant mortality – progress and problems. *Population Bulletin 31*:3.

Eckholm, Erik and F. Record
1976 *Two Faces of Malnutrition.* World Watch Paper No. 9, Washington, D.C.

Gavan, J.D.
1977 *Recent and Prospective Development in Food Consumption: Some Policy Issues.* International Food Policy Research Institute, Research Report 2, Washington, D.C.

Hopper, W.D.
1976 The development of agriculture in developing countries. *Scientific American 235:*197.

Janick, Jules, C.H. Noller, and C.L. Rhykerd
1976 The cycles of plant and animal nutrition. *Scientific American 235:*75.

McNamara, R.S.
1977 The Population Problem. Address to the Massachusetts Institute of Technology. International Bank for Reconstruction and Development, Washington, D.C.

Puffer, R.R., and C.V. Serrano
1973 *Nutritional Deficiency in Patterns of Mortality in Childhood.* Pan American Health Organization Scientific Publication No. 262, p. 161.

World Population Data Sheet
1978 Population Reference Bureau, Washington, D.C.

Wortman, Sterling
1976 Food and agriculture. *Scientific American 235:*31.

Breast Feeding And Infant Nutrition In Developing Countries

Derrick B. Jelliffe and E. F. Patrice Jelliffe

Infant feeding can best be understood as a nutritional, psychological, and biological interaction in which mother and offspring are mutually affected (Jelliffe & Jelliffe, 1978). It may be helpful to consider infant nutrition in terms of the early developmental stages of the human organism as classified by Bostock (1962) — that is, the fetus, the extero-gestate fetus (up to six or nine months postnatally), and the transitional (nine months to two or three years). An understanding of breast feeding and the infant's nutritional needs at each of these stages is important if effective measures against malnutrition in children of this age range are to be implemented.

The Fetus

Nutrition research endorses the truth of the old saying that "infant feeding begins in the uterus." Maternal nutrition prior to delivery affects the birth weight of the fetus and the levels of fetal stores of nutrients. A feeble, low birth weight baby starts a nutritionally hazardous life already at a disadvantage, with inadequate nutrient stores and probably deficient sucking vigor. In addition, the mother must lay down adequate lactation reserves during pregnancy, in the form of some 4 kilograms of subcutaneous fat, needed as a major source of calories and fatty acids for subsequent breast milk production.

In the developing countries, the level of maternal nutrition is affected by the cumulative impact of repeated reproductive cycles, often negatively compounded by hard work. Customs and practices in many cultures regulating the foods taken in pregnancy not infrequently limit the diet, often with a view to producing a small baby in the hope of an easier delivery. Such syndromes of "maternal depletion" (Berg, 1973), specific or general, are significant factors in unnecessary mortality in pregnancy and childbirth.

The Newborn

A great range of practices may be followed during childbirth in various cultures, many of significance to the well-being of both newborn and mother. For example, the time the umbilical cord is tied is of importance to the infant's iron stores.

[11]

The method in which the baby is put to the breast and the attitude towards colostrum (the mother's first milk secretion) are related to the ease (or otherwise) of initiation of lactation. The newborn is usually put to the breast very soon after delivery, and remains and sleeps by the mother's side. Colostrum is often regarded as important, and frequently is considered to have laxative properties. However, in a few communities, such as parts of northern Pakistan, colostrum was once considered to be poisonous and was expressed and discarded. In this situation, the newborn may be fed for a few days by a lactating relative or wet nurse, or given gruels, which often lead to potentially dangerous diarrhea. In parts of Malaysia, mashed ripe banana is fed to the breast-fed baby in the first days of life. Such "pre-lacteal feeds" are undertaken, in part, to "clean out" the meconium (the first fecal discharge by the newborn).

Culturally acceptable alternative sources of human milk when mothers die in childbirth have included lactating relatives, induced lactation, and employment of wet nurses. For example, among the Yoruba of Nigeria, a technique of inducing lactation was carried out using herbal remedies, massage to the breasts, and frequent suckling. Occasionally, if the mother died in childbirth, the situation of a newborn infant deprived of mother's milk (with no alternative source available) was considered hopeless in traditional communities; thus, the practice of burying the baby with the mother.

Breast Feeding

Breast milk was (and is) the bulwark of infant feeding for the extero-gestate fetus (especially the neonate) in non-Western cultures. Breast feeding is imperative if the survival of the baby is to be ensured.

Many cultures have various techniques and preparations, religious ceremonies, and rituals intended to stimulate the flow of breast milk, especially for the firstborn. Little scientific work has been undertaken in this matter. These methods often seem to be based on "sympathetic magic," with the use of milk-like substances or charms depicting large breasts (such as the Venus of Willendorf amulets), thereby reassuring the mother and enhancing the let-down reflex. For example, in ancient Polynesian Hawaii, prayers were made to the gods Ku and Hina, while strands of freshly plucked vine, dripping with milky sap, were hung on either side of the woman's chest. Although pharmacological effects may sometimes be responsible, it seems more likely that these procedures are more often confidence-inducing procedures – in modern parlance, reinforcers of the let-down reflex.

Traditional and modern dairy farmers have long known of the let-down reflex, appreciated only more recently by nutritionists as the psychosomatic key to the failure or success of breast feeding. The failure of the sophisticated, well-to-do urbanite with no knowledge and much apprehension, and of the shanty-town mother with the environmental psychosocial stress of her grim life, are both based in part on emotional interference with the let-down reflex (Jelliffe and Jelliffe, 1978). Conversely, the *doula*, or female assistant, is an active figure in pregnancy, childbirth, and the puerperium in social mammals (such as the dolphins) and in traditional human cultures (Raphael, 1973). She supplies physical and emotional support and information, and, above all, generates confidence. A *doula* effect is the reason for the success of spontaneous modern women's groups concerned with breast feeding such as the La Leche League International (LLLI) in the United States, the Nursing Mothers Association of Australia (NMAA), and Ammenhjelpen in Norway. They supply information and individual and group support through experienced mothers, and are, in fact, *doula*-surrogates.

Modern endocrinological research has also clarified the role of the prolactin reflex in successful breast feeding. It is often not appreciated that human prolactin was only isolated as recently as 1971 by Hwang and colleagues, who devised a method of radioimmunoassay (Hwang, Hardy, et al., 1971). Their research has led to much new work, particularly confirming the clinical observation that the greater the sucking stimulus – that is, the number of feedings, the length of feedings, and the vigor of the baby – the more milk secreted. The sucking stimulus directly affects prolactin secretion, which in turn stimulates milk production. Studies have also shown that prolactin plays multiple roles (Berg, 1973): inducing milk secretion in the mammary alveoli; promoting a water-conserving anti-diuretic effect in the kidneys; suppressing ovulation in the ovaries (anovulatory lactation amenorrhea); and, possibly, stimulating increased maternal behavior ("motherliness") through the central nervous system.

In non-Western cultures, the initiation and maintenance of lactation is usually successful and uncomplicated; close, continuing contact with the mother facilitates feeding at any time, place, or position during both day and night, thus ensuring maximal prolactin secretion. Close mothering is made easier in many cultures by traditional methods of baby-carrying.

Artificial feeding, usually for infants without available breast milk (particularly if the mother died in childbirth) has been used occasionally throughout history. Because of the inadequate nutritional composition of such feedings, often dilute animal milk or gruels, and associated diarrheal disease, babies fed in this way usually died. For example, in 1660 in England, over half the "hand reared" babies died in infancy, and their deaths were correctly labelled "died for want of breast milk." By contrast, only one-fifth of breast-fed babies died.

It is only in the past ten thousand years, following the domestication of various milk animals, that the possibility arose of using animal milk in infant feeding. People in various parts of the world have used the milk of many domesticated animals, including the cow, goat, sheep, buffalo, camel, yak, and the reindeer. Despite the fact that many different forms of feeding bowls (or cups, or horns) have been found in various archaeological sites, such forms of artificial feeding of babies were, for hygienic reasons, never practicable as a substitute for breast feeding.

The Extero-gestate Fetus

For the first six to nine months after birth, the baby can best be considered as an extero-gestate, or external, fetus, with the breast taking the place of the placenta. In non-Western cultures, those babies who survive the perils of birth trauma and neonatal infection usually do well in this phase of life on a diet of breast milk. Human milk is adapted to the specific needs of the neonate, particularly the characteristically rapid growth of the brain, and to protection against infection in the extero-gestate phase of life.

Despite this, infant mortality rates—that is, deaths during the first year of life—have been exceedingly high in most developing countries. These high rates have been in large measure from disease due to environmental and infective factors (such as respiratory infection, malaria, and accidents), together with infections and injuries associated with the birth process (such as tetanus, septicemia, and cerebral damage). Without breast feeding, infant mortality in developing countries reaches almost 100 percent, as can be seen in the extremely high mortality rate of artificially-fed babies in village circumstances, or in orphanages, even in the 1970's.

Patterns of feeding the extero-gestate fetus changed in the third quarter of the twentieth century, and new patterns of malnutrition are emerging. Shorter periods of adequacy of breast feeding appear to be becoming evident in women in some poorly-nourished communities, perhaps especially in urban slums. Infantile marasmus and diarrheal disease have increased as a result of inadequate lactation in poorly nourished mothers and, in some areas, as the side effects of estrogen-containing oral contraceptives contaminating the milk.

Conversely, in the developed countries, infantile obesity, or "protein-calorie malnutrition plus," is becoming a public health problem, and essentially is due to the practice of "double feeding," in which the baby is bottle fed, with the volume and concentration under the mother's control, and also receives an unnecessarily early introduction of semi-solid foods in the first weeks of life. Food allergy, particularly to cow's milk protein, is a rising concern due to such feeding patterns (Jelliffe and Jelliffe, 1978). Also, metabolic abnormalities in the early months of life, such as hypernatremia and aminoacidemia, are appearing.

Increasing industrialization in the developing countries, and the greater opportunities for women to work outside the home in urban areas, have been accompanied by an increase in bottle feeding. Rapid alterations in feeding behavior have been noted, for example, in Pakistani women who have migrated to Britain. The main factors responsible are undoubtedly social, cultural, and economic influences on the parents' attitudes and behavior in relation to their new self-image. The selection of life styles for new townsmen is much influenced by the example of the local elite, by the influence of advertising, and by the methods and procedures of health services. The example of Westerners living in developing countries, usually in cities, also seems to endorse artificial feeding. Breast feeding may be subconsciously equated with old-fashionedness, primitiveness and backwardness, while bottle feeding symbolizes urban life and therefore everything which is modern, scientific, and desirable.

The changing pattern of infant feeding in developing countries has led to profound alteration in the picture of child health. The main problems of health in developing countries in both mothers and their young offspring are related to three major factors: nutrition, infection, and hazardous, excessive pregnancies. When breast feeding is replaced by the inadequate bottle feeding found in developing countries, all of these factors are affected adversely, both for biological and economic reasons: nutrition deteriorates, infections (particularly diarrheal disease) increase, and pregnancies become more frequent, closely spaced, and hazardous, due to the loss of contraceptive protection afforded by lactation amenorrhea.

The size of the public health problems related to the availability (or otherwise) of human milk are huge, increasing, and almost completely unappreciated. All of the problems are worldwide, but are found in different patterns and proportions in different countries. For example, malnutrition and diarrheal disease affect children in disadvantaged communities in the developed countries; conversely, infantile obesity and cow's milk allergy affect the Westernized elite in newly developing nations.

In developing countries, it has been estimated that 9.4 million cases of severe protein-calorie malnutrition occur annually. The total number of infants suffering from kwashiorkor or from marasmus is not known. Assuming conservatively that only half of these cases suffer from marasmus related to bottle feeding or to inadequate lactation, this means that 4.7 million children could be protected, wholly or in part, by breast feeding from adequately fed mothers. The number of children with diarrhea associated with bottle feeding in such countries is difficult to calculate. However, the condition is common, and if a somewhat higher figure (5.3 million) than for marasmus is postulated, then the partial or complete protection of some 10 million infants may be available, simply by a return to breast feeding. With an assumed 30 percent mortality, this would mean three million lives saved, and with an arbitrary figure of one hundred U.S. dollars per child for treatment, a yearly expenditure of one billion dollars avoided.

From a family planning point of view, lactation amenorrhea associated with breast feeding currently affords 35 million couple-years protection annually, according to Rosa (1976); this is more protection than that achieved annually by technological contraceptives delivered through existing family planning services. Further decline in breast feeding will lead to a loss of this protection, an increase in birth rates, and the need for more funds and facilities to increase family planning services. If the trend toward bottle feeding in peri-urban areas of developing countries continues, it will lead to additional population increases of about 20 percent.

In an economic sense, Berg (1973) has calculated that if only one-fifth of the mothers in urban areas in developing countries do not breast feed, this represents a direct loss of 365 million dollars per year to these nations. What is more, this figure has to be doubled, at least in theory, to account for a similar expense in purchasing breast milk substitutes.

The Transitional Period

Breast feeding has an important child spacing function—to permit maturity of one child before the arrival of the next. The introduction of other foods seems to be signalled biologically by the readiness of the infant to deal with them, as judged by the appearance of "milk teeth," possibly by a rise of intestinal enzymes, and by an increase in manual dexterity.

The length of breast feeding and the culturally correct time for weaning, both in the sense of introducing other foods and of the stopping of breast feeding (*sevrage*), vary from one culture to another. The reason for *sevrage* is often a subsequent pregnancy; in some societies, particularly in parts of Africa, the birth-spacing effect of lactation amenorrhea is reinforced by sexual abstinence during the months of breast feeding. In other societies, the time for removal from the breast is defined by when a certain number of teeth have erupted, or the child can walk. However, in other societies, such as the San Blas Indians of Panama or the Karmajong of Uganda, breast feeding is continued throughout a subsequent pregnancy.

Generally, the weaning period's nutritional, infectious, and psychological dangers, and social significance, are clearly mirrored by the preference for certain seasons of the year (such as spring or fall in Europe), and by special ceremonies and *rites de passage*. Methods of separating the baby from the mother's milk vary considerably between cultures, as in the age at which it is undertaken, the suddenness, the "compensation" (if any), and the degree of physical separation of mother and child at the time.

The introduction of solid foods varies greatly. Sometimes, the pre-lacteal feedings commenced in the newborn period may be continued; softer items of the adult diet (or, less commonly, specially prepared items for young children) are introduced earlier or later in the second six months of life; or, solid foods may not be introduced until the second year of life.

All cultures have complex food classifications, which may limit the range of items available for infant feeding. In particular, foods considered appropriate or unsuitable for young children, the age at which they can be introduced, and the occurrence of ceremonies at these occasions, are all of importance to the infant's nutritional transition. The "cultural superfood" is of considerable significance. If this is low in protein and calories, and high in water and cellulose, such as yams or plantain, it places the transitional child at greater risk then in communities where a cereal grain (e.g., rice, wheat) is the cultural superfood. Cultural attitudes in infant feeding need to be considered in relation to their potential as "protein blocks"—that is, as practices which facilitate or make more difficult the use of locally available protein-rich foods.

For children in developing countries, weaning is the time of maximal nutritional stress. During the transitional period, the young child has to struggle to adjust to a variety of bacterial and parasitic infections, and often to the psychological trauma of separation from the mother's breasts. At the same time, the nutrient needs are high in view of the rapidity and complexity of growth and development, and the diet is likely to be inadequate in quantity, quality, and preparation. This is the period when "weanling diarrhea" principally occurs as an epidemiological entity in many societies, largely as a result of the interaction of malnutrition, intestinal infection, and ill-absorption of inadequately prepared new foods. It is also when kwashiorkor is particularly likely to develop if low protein foods are introduced, either with or without the continuance of small quantities of breast milk. It is the classical period for severe vitamin A deficiency, and for so-called "late marasmus," which, with increasing costs and scarcity of food supplies in many parts of the world, is probably on the increase.

In more affluent circumstances, little malnutrition is seen in this phase of life, except for obesity and the common problem of iron deficiency.

Culturally defined difficulties in persuading mothers to use available foods in the second semester of life have often been complicated by rising costs and more limited food supplies. In developing countries, the diet in this period should consist of as wide a range of mixtures of local foods as possible, with a small but significant volume of breast milk, often about a cupful a day. Such weaning foods should be prepared by following the concept of complementary protein "multi-mixes," basically often as a cereal-legume "double-mix," and with a realization that calories are needed as well as protein and other nutrients.

The role of commercially processed weaning foods varies. In rural areas of developing countries, they have little relevance. For the urban poor on a cash economy, they could play an important role, but are rarely geared to low budgets. In the developed countries, processed infant foods are widely used and forcefully promoted. They are convenient, but are usually poor buys in terms of nutrients. Indeed, their manufacturers are often more concerned with acceptability to the mother than with nutritional balance. In some of the more sophisticated developing countries, such as parts of the West Indies, such commercially prepared infant foods are being promoted for sale among poorer segments of the population, where their high cost and limited nutritional content make a negative contribution to the nutritional status of the local population.

Programmatic Considerations

The consequences of current patterns of infant feeding vary in importance in different parts of the world, notably with the prevalence and success of breast feeding and with the availability and use of suitable foods for the transitional child. Different as the problems of early childhood nutrition seem to be, the areas of emphasis in infant feeding are the same the world over, and there is no need for two standards, one for the affluent and another for the poor. Universally, the three main planks of scientifically guided, biologically optimal infant feeding should be: (1) to feed the pregnant and lactating mother with a mixed diet of locally available foods; (2) to feed the infant solely on breast milk for four to six months; and (3) to introduce least-cost weaning foods, based on the concept of "multimixes," from four to six months onwards, preferably prepared from locally available foods, but with continuing breast feeding into the second year of life, particularly for those in economically disadvantaged circumstances.

Such a regime would have a preventive effect of very great dimensions (table 2.1). For example, a return to more widespread breast feeding among urban women in developing countries can be estimated to protect some ten million infants affected each year by early marasmus and diarrheal disease. Conversely, continued breast feeding by women in developed countries could prevent about one million cases of infantile obesity and 100,000 cases of cow's milk allergy annually. These guidelines would also harmonize with the need to use local resources to best purpose and with least waste, and with the aim of national nutritional self-sufficiency.

The main need is for conviction on the part of the health professional, the economist, and the administrator. Programs to promote breast feeding in a community should be based on overall policy decisions. They should be interdisciplinary, and supported by funds for implementation and evaluation. Internationally concerned groups are slowly recognizing that such approaches are feasible and, in many areas, of the highest priority.

Concerning the transitional child, the situation remains largely the problem of convincing mothers in industrialized countries not to introduce semi-solids too early, and, in many developing countries, to introduce them

Table 2.1
SOME PROPHYLACTIC ADVANTAGES OF BREAST FEEDING

	DEVELOPING AREAS	DEVELOPED AREAS
(1) Nutrition	Marasmus + Diarrheal Disease (10 Million Cases/Year)	"Infantile Obesity" (1 Million Cases/Year) Metabolic Overload Syndrome
(2) Infections		Necrotizing Enterocolitis (?3500 Deaths/Year)
(3) Allergy	* * * * * *	Cow's Milk Allergy of Infancy (100,000 Cases/Year)
(4) Child Spacing	Highly Significant (More Protection Than Technological Programs)	Slight (With Widespread Technological Contraceptives)
(5) Economic Consequences	Billions of Dollars Needed Annually for Breast Milk Substitutes	

earlier—that is, in the second six months of life. Both are interwoven with cultural concepts: on the one hand, the desire for a "plump, healthy baby," and on the other, belief that such early use of foods is harmful to the infant for various reasons.

The question of free or subsidized supplementary feeding for children in the transitional phase of life needs consideration. Experience clearly indicates that supplementary feeding programs require careful consideration in the local context, with a policy appropriate to actual needs and resources. In famines and severe food shortages, this approach is obviously imperative. If suitable foods are available, but are not being used for cultural or biological reasons in infant feeding, such programs may be useless in counteracting infant malnutrition. Any scheme has to be realistically geared to actual circumstances in the area, including the presence or absence of health education, and must be designed with consideration for the future. There seems to be a trend in many areas towards the peripheral or village-level preparation of simply processed multi-mixes, based on local foods and available apparatus. These programs have the advantages of low cost, absence of transport problems, and built-in nutrition education potential.

Present day practices of infant feeding urgently require reappraisal. A system is needed based on a blend of modern scientific knowledge, awareness of successful traditional adaptations, and man's ancient biological/mammalian heritage.

References

Berg, A.
    1973   *The Nutrition Factor.* Brookings Institution, Washington, D.C.

Bostock, J.
    1962   Evolutionary approaches to infant care. *Lancet 1:*1033.

Hwang, P., J. Hardy, H. Friesen, and D. Whansky
    1971   Biosynthesis of human growth hormone and prolactin by normal
                pituitary glands and pituitary adenomas. *Journal of Clinical
                Endocrinology and Metabolism 33*:1.

Jelliffe, D. B.
    1968   *Infant Nutrition in the Subtropics and Tropics.* 2nd ed. World Health
                Organization Monograph No. 29, Geneva.

Jelliffe, D. B., and E. F. P. Jelliffe
    1978   *Human Milk in the Modern World.* Oxford University Press, New York.

Raphael, D.
    1973   *The Tender Gift: Breast Feeding.* Prentice-Hall, Englewood Cliffs, New
                Jersey.

Rosa, F.
    1976   Breast feeding and family planning. *PAG Bulletin 5:*5.

Nutrition, Infection, And Immunity

Otto F. Sieber, Jr., and Glenn Lippman

Nutrition has been a high priority health concern in developing countries for many years. Since the original descriptions of protein-calorie malnutrition in West Africa in the 1920's and 1930's (Williams, 1933), the overwhelming mortality and morbidity from malnutrition and the resultant loss of human resources has provided the major impetus for dedicating large portions of limited national resources toward improving the health of infants and children. It had been hoped that such programs as nutritional supplementation and the encouragement of breast feeding would reduce death and morbidity. Although nutrition may be improving in certain areas of the world, these goals have not yet been attained for the world at large.

For a country such as the U.S., the nutrition picture obviously has not been the same. Gross nutritional abnormalities because of malnutrition were felt not to be a general problem, but limited to the developing countries or to members of low socio-economic communities. The result has been that nutrition has not been viewed as a legitimate field of broad primary medical concern or even education within the practicing medical community in the U.S.

A focus is needed within the fields of both public health and the private practice of medicine which would permit the development of a legitimate, broadly based, medically-related nutrition program. Historically, the discovery and use of vitamins provided needed direction for the nutritional and medical programs of an earlier period in medicine. Vitamin deficiencies, their diagnosis and treatment, were obviously of importance for both public health and primary care providers, and the objectives of improving nutrition, diagnosing and treating deficiency states, and preventing such deficiencies were achieved. In the ensuing period (1940-1960), subsequent emphasis on subspecialization turned the medical community away from interest in general nutrition, and, until recently, nutrition was seen by physicians largely in terms of either public health programs or more basic bio-chemical abnormalities.

Interest in nutrition appeared to be increasing again in the 1970's. Contributing to this may be the emphasis in medical education and medical practice on primary and preventive care, a reflection of the 1920's – 1930's era, when preventive and therapeutic medicine worked so closely together.

Coinciding with this resurgence of primary care in medical care programs has been an interest in the changes in immune function induced by inadequate nutrition, leading to, or aggravated by, serious infection. The observations that functional changes occur in the ability of the malnourished human host to respond to infection, and that these changes correlate with the intake of specific nutrients, such as protein, vitamins, iron, and zinc, is somewhat analogous to the earlier recognition of vitamins and their role in vitamin deficiency diseases. Just as the medical community of that period provided primary care in diagnosing and treating vitamin deficiencies, and the public health and governmental sectors provided the national resources for research and preventive measures, immunology of the malnourished person can provide a similar focus. We are entering a time when cooperation between all levels of government and the medical community must exist; malnutrition is not limited to developing countries, nor are the means to understand the mechanisms of the effect of malnutrition on the host, or the measures to treat or prevent those abnormalities, limited to any one region of the world.

An understanding of immunity and malnutrition will permit closer professional relationships to develop between the practitioner of medicine, the public health worker, the nutritionist, the student, and others for whom nutrition will be a significant concern in the years ahead.

Protein-Calorie Malnutrition

Moderate to severe protein-calorie malnutrition may effect 20-30 percent of the infants and children in the developing world (Bengoa, 1975), and may contribute to as much as 50 percent of this population's mortality (Pan American Health Organization, 1971). Although this degree of malnutrition is much less common in the U.S. (Owen et al., 1974; Owen & Lippman, 1977), one of the common factors associated with malnutrition – poverty – is certainly present in this country. Of more nutritional significance in the U.S. may be the entity of subclinical, or mild to moderate, malnutrition (Robson, 1972). Indeed, the observations that significant malnutrition may appear rapidly in "normal" health care delivery situations, such as pediatric care (John et al., 1976; Brown, 1977), or with debilitated or hospitalized patients (Bollet & Owens, 1973; Prevost & Butterworth, 1974; Bistrian et al., 1974; Bistrian et al. 1977), support this concern.

The clinical expression of the observable malnourished state is most clearly defined in the infant or child. The expression of malnutrition varies with the amount of nutrients lost from the diet, and is related to the proportion of calories lost from the diet due to decreased carbohydrate or decreased protein intake, or the combined loss of these nutrients (figure 3.1). Marasmus and kwashiorkor in infants and children may be delineated by clinical appearance

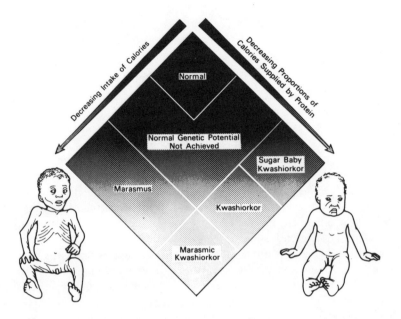

Fig. 3.1

alone, but the syndromes can also be defined biochemically and anthropometrically.

The distinctions between various types of malnourished states usually are not clear-cut, and combinations of findings between marasmus and kwashiorkor often may be seen. In addition, there is as yet a large area of mild to moderate malnutrition which is difficult to detect clinically, but which may be measurable in terms of unachieved immunological, neurological, or genetic potential. Malnutrition which occurs prenatally or in the early postnatal period has been suggested to affect brain growth and presumably intellectual functioning (Voorhees et al., 1975; Winick, 1976). Observations that nutritional status has an effect on the host beyond that on visible growth and development have renewed interest in nutritional status in developed as well as developing countries.

Significantly, the nutritional status of a human being may also affect the ability of that host to respond to infection. This effect of nutrition appears to be mediated through the host's immune system, and although the relation between infection and nutritional deficiency has been recognized for some time, it is only recently that specific abnormalities in the immune system have been correlated with nutritional deficiencies. This has already been the subject of extensive reviews (Faulk et al., 1974; Chandra and Newberne, 1977; Suskind, 1977).

Normal Immune Function

The human host has numerous ways of combatting infection. These defensive responses are selective, sequential, and rate-dependent upon whether the host is being challenged by the infectious agent for the first time or recognizes the challenge from a previous exposure.

The first line of defense against any infectious challenge is the providing of effective barriers. This defense is related to the integrity of an individual's skin, as well as the cellular makeup and availability of protective secretions in the respiratory tract (eyes, nose, mouth) and intestinal tract (Sirisinha et al., 1975; Neumann et al., 1975).

Appropriate defensive immunological responses which occur following penetration of an infectious agent into a host depend upon the interplay between cells and cell products. Infectious agents are eliminated from the body by a number of mechanisms, which include ingestion by specialized cells (leukocytes and macrophages), and killing by antibody, complement, and other cell products (produced by such cells as lymphocytes). Mechanisms of elimination will vary according to the infectious agent invading the host. The development and functioning of the immune system is reviewed by Bellanti (1978).

In understanding the implications of malnutrition on immune function, the complexity of the immune system must be appreciated. Simply stated, the maturation of immunologically active cells begins with a single cell type, the stem cell, present in the bone marrow of the fetus. The stem cell follows one of two pathways to become a fully functional contributor to the immune response. One of these, the B cell, leads to the development of plasma cells, important in the production of antibodies and immunoglobulins. The other pathway requires processing of the stem cell by the thymus prior to differentiation of the second major lymphocyte type, the T or thymus cell. Functionally, T cells contribute to delayed hypersensitivity, one commonly known expression of which is in the skin test reaction. T cell lymphocytes are associated with defenses against viruses, fungi, mycobacteria, and parasites by a mechanism termed "cell-mediated immunity." B cell lymphocytes produce immunoglobulins of various types and function in response to stimulation by specific organisms. Mediation of immune function also occurs between the B and T cells through effector molecules produced by the T lymphocyte.

Effects of Malnutrition on Infectious Diseases

Because of the immunological changes observed with malnutrition, the undernourished child is more severely affected by illness than the adequately fed child (Scrimshaw et al., 1968; Gordon & Scrimshaw, 1970; Purtilo & Connor, 1975). Diseases caused by organisms which are controlled by the cell-mediated immune T cell system seem to predominate; these include measles, influenza, tuberculosis, malaria, chickenpox, rubella, and conditions caused by herpes simplex virus, *Pseudomonas aeruginosa*, *Pneumocystis carinii*, and *Candida albicans* (Wiley & Maverakis, 1968; Scrimshaw et al., 1968; Purtilo & Connor, 1975). The malnourished host is not only predisposed to infection with the above-mentioned agents, but also experiences a variation from the usual expression and clinical course of the disease. A febrile response to infection is less common in the malnourished patient. Infection with pyogenic organisms such as *Streptococcus pneumoniae* tends to be associated with gangrene rather than suppuration. Malnourished children with exanthematous diseases such as measles have a lowered frequency of rash, and a six-fold higher incidence of pneumonia, in comparison to better nourished children (Smythe et al., 1971). Infections tend to spread from their initial site, with dissemination throughout the host.

It should be emphasized here that there are other conditions which produce patterns of infection similar to those just described. Abnormal responses to infection are also seen in the cancer patient treated with immunosuppressive agents (Chandra & Newberne, 1977; Richie & Copeland, 1978), the severely burned individual with skin and tissue damage (Chandra & Newberne, 1977), and the premature infant with an immature immune system (Wilson & Eichenwald, 1974).

Since infection is frequent among children in developing countries, prevention of infection would be likely to lessen the incidence and severity of frank malnutrition precipitated by disease in those individuals who are in borderline nutritional balance. In planning policies, the use of immunizing agents must be balanced against all other demands on limited monetary resources. However, it should be remembered that the efficacy of vaccines has been determined from studies with well-nourished children, and must be critically re-evaluated when being applied to malnourished children. For example, when smallpox was a major public health problem, occasional cases of progressive vaccinia would occur because of the failure of the immune system to properly mediate the vaccination and control the spread of the virus (Suskind, 1977). Also, polio virus vaccine has a different effect in someone who is malnourished than in a well-nourished host. As a result of such findings, several research centers are attempting to determine the relationship between immunization and nutritional status.

Not only may the expected results of an immunization procedure change, but it is possible that the immunization may have a catabolic effect on the recipient's nutritional status. It appears that if the vaccine challenge and the host response are spread out over a period of time, the catabolic effect on a malnourished child is minimized. If, however, the response to immunization occurs over a short period of time (less than eight days), the caloric penalty is severe enough that it would be possible that immunization could precipitate a kwashiorkor state in a patient with borderline nutrition (Kielman, 1977).

Effects of Malnutrition on Immune Function

Protein-calorie malnutrition may induce an acquired immunodeficiency state, with resultant increases in frequency and severity of infection. This condition has been well described in malnourished infants in developing countries (Pan American Health Organization, 1971), but is being described with increasing frequency in developed countries as well (John et al., 1976). It is of milder and more moderate severity in developed countries and in varying age groups, including adults (Bistrian et al., 1974; Butterworth, 1974). The catabolic effects of hospitalization and illness, in the face of inadequate nutritional support, produce a syndrome in adults with changes in immune function similar to those in children (Law, 1973; Bistrian et al., 1977).

Figure 3.2 indicates the nutritional and immunological effects of an infectious respiratory disease, pertussis (whooping cough). In a three month old infant with a risk factor, such as prematurity and failure to thrive, the mechanical interference of paroxysmal coughing with eating decreases calorie and protein intake to the extent that frank malnutrition results. This has been shown to be associated with a change in immunological functioning and

RELATIONS OF MALNUTRITION, INFECTION AND IMMUNE RESPONSE

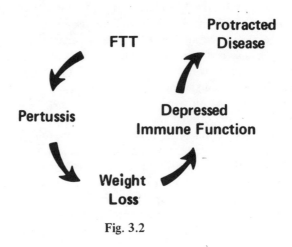

Fig. 3.2

prolongation of the clinical disease, unresponsive to therapy other than nutritional reconstitution (Sieber & Harrison, 1979).

The degree of immunological derangement is not predictable from the degree of malnutrition. It occurs selectively and at several levels; however, the humoral component of the immune system remains relatively intact (Reddy & Srikantia, 1964; Brown & Katz, 1966; Jose et al., 1970; Alvarado & Luthringer, 1971; Sirisinha et al., 1973). Figure 3.3 suggests a mechanism by which the sparing of immunoglobulins in the malnourished patient is related

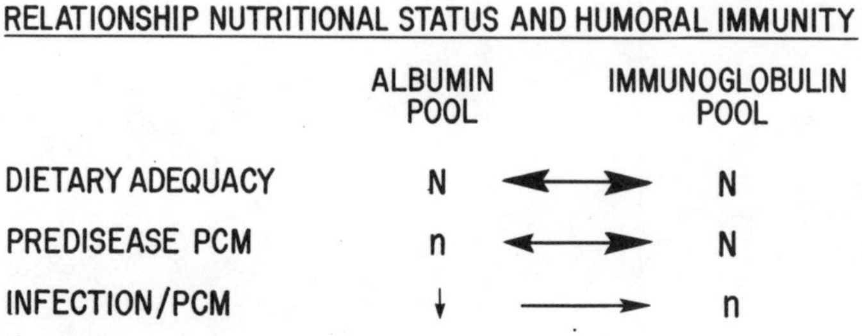

RELATIONSHIP NUTRITIONAL STATUS AND HUMORAL IMMUNITY

	ALBUMIN POOL		IMMUNOGLOBULIN POOL
DIETARY ADEQUACY	N	←——→	N
PREDISEASE PCM	n	←——→	N
INFECTION/PCM	↓	——→	n

Fig. 3.3

to the balance between the albumin pool and the non-albumin (immunoglobulin) protein pool and the amount of exogenous protein repletion. Only when primary immune responses are involved has there been evidence of functional IgM abnormality, despite approximately normal levels in non-infected malnourished subjects (Lechtig et al., 1970; Law et al., 1973).

Table 3.1 summarizes the specific effects of malnutrition on all immunological parameters. In some reports, serum IgA and IgE levels have been increased. No allergic symptoms have appeared when this is noted. Except for C_4, complement levels decrease in all forms of malnutrition (Hafez et al., 1977; Razban et al., 1975; McFarlane, 1976). However, it is unclear whether these changes reflect decreased synthesis or increased utilization in the face of intercurrent infection.

The most significant change in the immune system related to malnutrition is in cell mediated immunity (CMI). The total number of lymphocytes involved in this response are reduced (Geefhuysen et al., 1971). The subpopulation of cells, i.e., the proportion of T cells, is decreased and there is a functional diminution in the manner in which these cells recognize and respond to foreign matter or organisms (Douglas & Schopfer, 1976; Kulapongs et al., 1977). One measure of CMI function is in skin test reactivity, which is complex and requires the interaction of the T cell with other cell types; such reactivity is diminished or lost in malnutrition (Geefhuysen et al., 1971; Kulapongs et al., 1977). In addition to functional changes, anatomical changes may also be observed in thymic tissue (atrophy

Table 3.1

IMMUNOLOGICAL EFFECTS OF MALNUTRITION

FUNCTIONAL EFFECT	IMMUNOLOGICAL PARAMETERS			
	INNATE	HUMORAL	CELL MEDIATED	PHAGOCYTIC
INCREASE		IgG IgA IgE		
NO CHANGE	Chemotaxis NBT reduction	Lymph node germinal centers Circulating "B" cells Function of "B" cells Plasma cell function Specific antibodies		Bacterial killing Intracellular enzymes Phagocytosis Polymorphonuclear numbers
DECREASE	Complement Interferon production Rebuck window	IgM IgG-Late Secretory IgA Specific Antibodies	Thymus size Lymph node size Lymph node cortex Circulating "T" cells Lymphocyte blastogenesis Skin tests Effector molecules	Opsonins Oxidative metabolism

and involution) and lymph nodes (paracortical depletion) (Mugerwa, 1971; Smythe et al., 1971; Douglas & Schopfer, 1976; Schopfer & Douglas, 1976).

The effects of nutritional status on immune function vary in degree and duration with the age at which nutritional deficiency occurs for a host. Intrauterine growth retardation appears to affect the immune system to as great a degree and with the same permanence (Aref et al., 1970; Chandra, 1975; Chandra, 1977) as it effects neurological growth and postnatal functioning (Winick, 1976). Since malnutrition is known to produce atrophy of the thymus and lymph tissues (Mugerwa, 1971; Jackson, 1925), immunological consequences might be anticipated in a number of body defense functions (Katz and Stiehm, 1977) should the immune system be deprived of adequate nutrients during its formative period. However, phagocytic cell and B cell function are less affected than T cell function and complement activity (table 3.1). For the infant with intrauterine growth retardation, decreases in numbers of lymphocytes in the perinatal period appear to be corrected by age five years. However, physiological abnormalities such as decreased lymphocyte reactivity and skin test reactivity persist (Chandra, 1977; Ferguson, 1978).

Changes similar to those observed *in utero* occur when malnutrition is imposed on a functional immune system at a later age (Smythe et al., 1971). These changes, however, are less permanent and more correctible if the malnutrition occurs after six to eight months of age (Chandra, 1977).

Pharmacologic Effects of Malnutrition

It was reported in the 1970's that nutritional status, as determined by both the amount of dietary protein and the quantity of that protein, can alter the rate of metabolizing certain pharmacologic agents in the malnourished individual. Because infection occurs so frequently in malnourished patients, optimal antimicrobial therapy may be difficult to achieve without knowledge of an individual's nutritional state. Animal studies dealing with a variety of pharmacologic agents have demonstrated nutritionally-induced alterations of enzymatic drug metabolism, which reflect alterations in metabolic pathways (Dixon et al., 1960; Kato & Takanada, 1967; Kato, 1967; Hospador & Manthei, 1968; Boyd & Chen, 1968; Boyd & Castro, 1968; Kato et al., 1968; Weatherholz et al., 1969; Furner & Feller, 1971).

Studies on human subjects have produced conflicting data. In one study, the metabolism of chloramphenicol was altered in malnourished children, leading to longer clearance times and increased peak plasma levels (Mehta et al., 1975). Slower biotransformation of the drug, resulting from malnutrition-induced changes in liver enzyme activity, suggest that reductions in dosage regimes for such children should be considered. However, Buchanan (1977) demonstrated that protein binding of chloramphenicol in malnourished children was approximately 5 percent below controls, although relatively large amounts of free drug were in the circulation (75 percent in controls verus 80 percent in children with kwashiorkor).

Clearance rates of tetracycline hydrochloride are also increased in malnourished children, with protein binding and the volume of distribution decreased when compared with control groups (Shastri & Krishnaswamy, 1976; Raghuram & Krishnaswamy, 1977). For this antibiotic, the dosage frequency should perhaps be increased in malnourished children for optimal effectiveness. Changes in antibiotic metabolism with kwashiorkor have also been noted with the antimalarial, chloroquine (Buchanan & Van der Walt, 1977). Serum binding switches from albumin to gamma globulin because gamma globulin is spared relative to the changes in albumin synthesis resulting from malnutrition. Streptomycin (Buchanan, 1977) has also been shown to have decreased protein binding in patients with protein-calorie malnutrition. It may be speculated that toxicity could result from increased amounts of such freely circulating drug.

The abnormalities of metabolism previously discussed are not limited to individuals residing in developing countries. Studies of patient populations in both university and county hospitals in the U.S. have identified postsurgical and debilitated individuals whose biochemical makeup mimics acute protein-calorie malnutrition (Bollet & Owens, 1973; Prevost & Butterworth, 1974). Because of this, further examination of the methodology used to estimate drug dosage in the malnourished patient is needed. Demonstrations of abnormal protein binding and hepatic transformation may indicate that the use of a standard "dose per kilogram" may be inappropriate, and that a dosage schedule reflecting the nutritional status of the patient should be evolved, as well. Such findings in patient populations also suggest that the need for wider-scale supplemental feeding programs in the U.S. should be closely examined.

Therapeutic Uses of Nutrition

The identification of malnutrition in individuals, as well as in populations from both developed and developing countries, should promote the standardization of nutritional assessment techniques and knowledge for practitioners in clinical, epidemiological, and public health areas. Broadened use of the skills and the medical knowledge required for their use potentially increase the benefits from nutrition programs. Such programs will contribute not only to the preventive approach to nutritional inadequacies, but also to the therapeutic approach.

Optimal use of currently available nutritional therapeutic modalities, such as elemental diets and hyperalimentation, requires improved skills and knowledge to promote their more timely application to patient needs.

Anticipation of the need for nutritional support must be emphasized and will require better definition of risk factors for patients in all socioeconomic categories. Table 3.2 summarizes those risk factors which may be associated with infection in the malnourished child or adult, and which can be used to identify the individual in need of additional nutritional surveillance, evaluation, and support.

The presence of infections known to require cell-mediated immunity for their control should suggest a need for nutritional assessment of the patient. Functional abnormalities of lymphatic cells persisting after some minor degree of nutritional reconstitution require more evaluation of the extent of disease, and may require aggressive nutritional support.

Perhaps there are limitations to the expectations which can result from nutritional programs at national levels. Alternative measures of dealing with and breaking the malnutrition-infection cycle have been suggested and are beginning to show advantages over large-scale nutrition intervention programs. Nutritional supplementation alone may not prevent all malnutrition and its severe effects on immune responsiveness. Anti-parasitic programs on a large scale may provide nutritional benefits to the host in lieu of the more common emphasis on supplementing the diet to modify malnutrition (Suskind, 1977).

There appears to be yet another consideration in influencing or modifying nutritional programs, namely, the concept of immunologic manipulation, provided in addition to nutritional supplementation. One such example (Faulk & Jose, 1977) suggests that when transfer factor therapy is added to nutritional replenishment in the malnourished patient, at a time when nutritional rejuvenation has been accomplished, protection against relapse from diarrheal disease is enhanced. This compares to no improvement when either transfer factor is administered in the acute stage of malnutrition with infection (prior to nutritional reconstitution), or when nutritional replenishment alone is provided.

The net effect of these considerations is that the nutrition programs of both developed and developing countries must be similar, requiring both clinical crisis intervention and food supplement programs for optimal effectiveness. The programs differ only in the percent of emphasis to be placed on either of these areas (figure 3.4). The recognition that there is a common denominator between nutritional problems in developed and developing countries permits improved utilization of limited resources and a broader base of discussion and action for health care delivery specialists.

Conclusion
Nutritional sciences are entering an era in which they will play many roles in medicine. Agriculture will attempt to increase production of proven foodstuffs, as well as to foster new sources of protein. This effort may

Table 3.2

**RISK FACTORS ASSOCIATED WITH INFECTION IN THE
MALNOURISHED INDIVIDUAL**

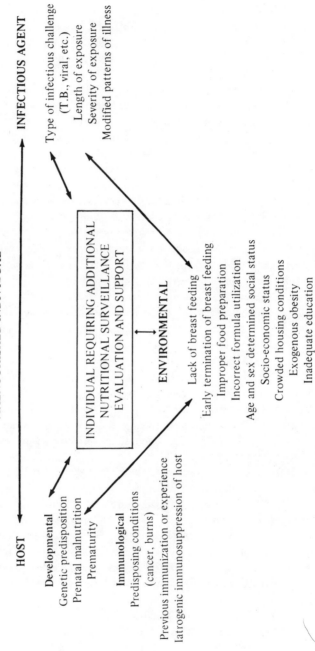

HOST

Developmental
Genetic predisposition
Prenatal malnutrition
Prematurity

Immunological
Predisposing conditions
(cancer, burns)
Previous immunization or experience
Iatrogenic immunosuppression of host

INDIVIDUAL REQUIRING ADDITIONAL
NUTRITIONAL SURVEILLANCE
EVALUATION AND SUPPORT

ENVIRONMENTAL

Lack of breast feeding
Early termination of breast feeding
Improper food preparation
Incorrect formula utilization
Age and sex determined social status
Socio-economic status
Crowded housing conditions
Exogenous obesity
Inadequate education

INFECTIOUS AGENT

Type of infectious challenge
(T.B., viral, etc.)
Length of exposure
Severity of exposure
Modified patterns of illness

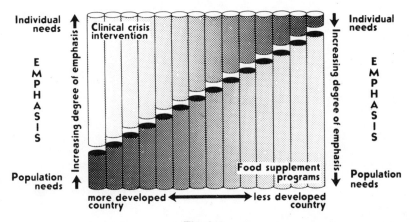

Fig. 3.4

provide the means to improve nutrition for all, thereby decreasing gross malnutrition. However, malnutrition in various forms will continue to occur, and when it occurs at significant times throughout life, such as *in utero,* it will continue to create serious sequelae.

For the individual with acute malnutrition, as has been observed for the elderly hospital patient or the child with acute infection, functional effects of malnutrition must continue to be looked for and recognized. They will require specific treatment and nutritional support. For the clinician or health associate, malnutrition must be recognized as a cause of acquired immunosuppression, potentially leading to opportunistic infection. Preventive measures, such as immunizations, must be evaluated in light of the nutritional state of the host, and parameters must be defined in which immunizations will have an optimal effect. Perhaps clinical or biochemical nutritional screens, such as serum albumin levels, will provide guidance for the vaccination of children in at-risk populations, since a normal albumin level is associated with a good potential for antibody production (Suskind, 1977).

Food support programs for populations with poor nutrition, whether in the U.S. urban ghetto or in a developing country, should be considered carefully. Food supplementation, by itself, may have to be modified in favor of support programs which consider various other factors. The current level of knowledge concerning the interaction of nutritional status with infectious disease points to the need for these divergent programs.

References

Alvarado, J., and D.G. Luthringer
  1971   Serum immunoglobulins in edematous protein-calorie malnourished children. *Clinical Pediatrics 10:*174.

Aref, G.H., M.K. Badr el Din, A.I. Hassan, and I.I. Araby
     1970   Immunoglobulins in kwashiorkor. *Journal of Tropical Medicine and Hygiene 73:*186.

Bellanti, J.A.
     1978   *Immunology II.* Saunders, Philadelphia.

Bengoa, J.M.
     1973   Prevention of protein-calorie malnutrition. In *Protein Calorie Malnutrition,* Robert E. Olson, ed., Academic Press, New York, p. 435.

Bistrian, B.R., G.L. Blackburn, E. Hallowell, and R. Heddle
     1974   Protein status of general surgical patients. *Journal of American Medical Association 230:*858.

Bistrian, B.R., M. Sherman, G.L. Blackburn, R. Marshall, and C. Shaw
     1977   Cellular immunity in adult marasmus. *Archives of Internal Medicine 137:*1408.

Bollet, A.J., and S. Owens
     1973   Evaluation of nutritional status of selected hospital patients. *American Journal of Clinical Nutrition 26:*931.

Boyd, E.M., and E.S. Castro
     1968   Protein-deficient diet and DDT toxicity. *Bulletin of the World Health Organization 38:*141.

Boyd, E.M., and C.P. Chen
     1968   Lindane toxicity and protein-deficient diet. *Archives of Environmental Health 17:*156.

Brown, R.E.
     1977   Interaction of nutrition and infection in clinical practice. *Pediatric Clinics of North America 24:*241.

Brown, R.E., and M. Katz
     1966   Failure of antibody production to yellow fever vaccine in children with kwashiorkor. *Tropical and Geographic Medicine 18:*125.

Buchanan, N.
     1977   The binding of antituberculous drugs to normal and kwashiorkor serum. *South African Medical Journal 52*(13):522.

Buchanan, N., and L. Van der Walt
     1977   Chloramphenicol binding to normal and kwashiorkor sera. *American Journal of Clinical Nutrition 30:*847.

Butterworth, C.E., Jr.
     1974   Malnutrition in the hospital. *Journal of the American Medical Association 230:*879.

Chandra, R.K.
     1975   Fetal malnutrition and postnatal immunocompetence. *American Journal of Diseases of Childhood 129:*450.

Chandra, R.K.
     1977   Immunoglobulins and Antibody Response in Protein-Calorie Malnutrition — A Review. In *Malnutrition and the Immune Response,* R.M. Suskind, ed., Raven Press, New York, p. 155.

Chandra, R.K., and P.M. Newberne
     1977   *Nutrition, Immunity, and Infection: Mechanisms of interactions.* Plenum Press, New York.

Dixon, R., R. Shultice, and J. Fouts
     1960   Factors affecting drug metabolism by liver microsomes. IV. Starvation (25509). *Proceedings of Society for Experimental Biology and Medicine 103:*333.

Douglas, S.D., and K. Schopfer
     1976   Analytical review: Host defense mechanisms in protein-energy malnutrition. *Clinical Immunology and Immunopathology 5:*1.

Dudrick, S.J., J.M. Long, E. Steiger, and J.E. Rhoads
1970   Intravenous hyperalimentation. *Medical Clinics of North America*
           *54:*577.

Edelman, R.
1977   Cell-mediated immune response in protein-calorie malnutrition – a
           review. In *Malnutrition and the Immune Response,* R.M. Suskind, ed,
           Raven Press, New York, p. 47.

Faulk, W.P., E.M. Demaeyer, and A.J.S. Davies
1974   Some effects of malnutrition on the immune response in man.
           *American Journal of Clinical Nutrition 27:*638.

Faulk, W.P., and D.G. Jose
1977   *Nutrition and Immunity Workshop. Progress in Immunology.*
           Proceedings of the Third International Congress of Immunology.
           Australian Academy of Science, Elsener/North Holland.

Ferguson, A.C.
1978   Prolonged impairment of cellular immunity in children with
           intrauterine growth retardation. *Journal of Pediatrics 93:*52.

Furner, R.L. and D.D. Feller
1971   The influence of starvation upon hepatic drug metabolism in rats, mice
           and guinea pigs. *Proceedings of the Society for Experimental Biology
           and Medicine 137:*816.

Geefhuysen, J., E. Rosen, J. Katz, T. Ipp, and J. Metz
1971   Impaired cellular immunity in kwashiorkor with improvement after
           therapy. *British Medical Journal 4:*527.

Gordon, J.E. and N.S. Scrimshaw
1970   Infectious disease in the malnourished. *Medical Clinics of North
           America 54:*1495.

Hafez, M., G.H. Aref, S.N. Mehareb, A.H. Kassem, H. El-Tahhan, Z. Risk, R. Mahfouz,
and K. Saad
1977   Antibody production and complement system in protein energy
           malnutrition. *Journal of Tropical Medicine and Hygiene 80:*36.

Hospador, M. and R. Manthei
1968   Influence of age and diet on the induction of hexobarbital-metabolizing
           enzymes in the mouse. *Proceedings of Society for Experimental
           Biology and Medicine 128:*130.

Jackson, C.M.
1925   *The Effects of Inanition and Malnutrition upon Growth and Structure.*
           McGraw-Hill Book Company, Philadelphia.

John, T.J., J. Blazovich, E.S. Lightner, O.F. Sieber, Jr., J.J. Corrigan and R. Hansen
1976   Kwashiorkor not associated with poverty. *Journal of Pediatrics 90:*730.

Jose, D.G., J.S. Welch, and R.L. Doherty
1970   *Australian Pediatrics Journal 6:*192.

Jose, D.G., O. Stutman, and R.A. Good
1973   Long term effects on immune function of early nutritional deprivation.
           *Nature 241:*57.

Kato, R.
1967   Effect of phenobarbital treatment on the activities of nadph-dependent
           enzymes of liver microsomes in fasted or sucrose fed rats. *Japanese
           Journal of Pharmacy 18:*356.

Kato, R., T. Oshima, and S. Tomizawa
1968   Toxicity and metabolism of drugs in relation to dietary protein.
           *Japanese Journal of Pharmacology 18:*356.

Kato, R., and A. Takanaka
1967   Effect of starvation on the *in vivo* metabolism and effect of drugs in
           female and male rats. *Japanese Journal of Pharmacy 17:*208.

Katz, M., and R.E. Stiehm
    1977   Host defense in malnutrition. *Pediatrics 59:*490.

Kielmann, A.A.
    1977   Nutritional and immune responses of subclinically malnourished Indian
                children. In *Malnutrition and the Immune Response,* R.M. Suskind, ed.,
                Raven Press, New York, p. 429.

Kulapongs, P., R. Edelman, R. Suskind, and R.E. Olson
    1977   Defective local leukocyte mobilization in children with kwashiorkor.
                *American Journal of Clinical Nutrition 30:*367.

Law, D.K., S.J. Dudrick, and N.I. Abdou
    1973   Immunocompetence of patients with protein-calorie malnutrition. The
                effects of nutritional repletion. *Annals of Internal Medicine 79:*545.

Lechtig, A., G. Arroyave, F. Viteri, and L. J. Mata
    1970   *Archives of Latin American Nutrition 20:*321.

McFarlane, H.
    1976   Malnutrition and impaired immune response to infection. *Proceedings
                of the Nutritional Society 35:*263.

Mehta, S., H.K. Kalsi, S. Jayaraman, and V.S. Mathur
    1975   Chloramphenicol metabolism in children with protein-calorie
                malnutrition. *American Journal of Clinical Nutrition 28:*977.

Mugerwa, J.W.
    1971   The lymphoreticular system in kwashiorkor. *Journal of Pathology
                105:*105.

National Academy of Science
    1976   *Immune Response of the Malnourished Child:* A position paper of the
                Food and Nutrition Board of the National Council.

Neumann, C., G.J. Lawlor, Jr., E.R. Stiehm, M.E. Swendseid, C. Newton, J. Herbert,
A.J. Ammann, and M. Jacob
    1975   Immunologic responses in malnourished children. *American Journal of
                Clinical Nutrition 28:*89.

Olusi, S.O., and H. McFarlane
    1976   Effects of early protein-calorie malnutrition on the immune response.
                *Pediatric Research 10:*707.

Owen, G.M., K.M. Kram, P.J. Garry, J.E. Lowe, and A.H. Lubin
    1974   A study of nutritional status of preschool children in the United States,
                1968-1970. *Pediatrics 53:*597.

Owen, G., and G. Lippman
    1977   Nutritional status of infants and young children: U.S.A. *Pediatric
                Clinics of North America 24:*211.

Pan American Health Organization
    1971   *Inter-American Investigation of Mortality in Childhood. First Year of
                Investigation, Provisional Report.* Pan American Health Organization,
                Washington, D.C.

Prevost, E.A. and C.E. Butterworth
    1974   Nutritional care of hospitalized patients. *Clinical Research 22:*579A.

Purtilo, D.T. and D.H. Connor
    1975   Fatal infections in protein-calorie malnourished children with
                thymolymphatic atrophy. *Archives of Disease in Childhood 50:*149.

Raghuram, T.C., and K. Krishnaswamy
    1977   Influence of nutritional status on plasma levels and relative
                bioavailability of tetracycline. *European Journal of Clinical
                Pharmacology 12:*281.

Razban, S.Z., S.O. Olushi, M.A. Ade-Serrano, B.O. Osunkoya, H.A. Adeshina, and H.
McFarlane
    1975   Acute phase proteins in children with protein-calorie malnutrition.
                *Journal of Tropical Medicine and Hygiene 78:*264.

Reddy, V. and S.G. Srikantia
1964   Antibody response in kwashiorkor. *Indian Journal of Medical Research* *52*:1154.

Richie, E. and E.M. Copeland
1978   *Cancer Bulletin 30:*78.

Robson, J.R.
1972   *Malnutrition: Its Causation and Control.* Gordon and Breach, New York.

Schopfer, K., and S.D. Douglas
1976   In vitro studies of lymphocytes from children with kwashiorkor. *Clinical Immunology and Immunopathology 5:* 21.

Scrimshaw, N.S., C.E. Taylor, and J.E. Gordon
1968   *Interactions of Nutrition and Infection.* World Health Organization, Geneva.

Shastri, R.A. and I. Krishnaswamy
1976   Undernutrition and tetracycline half life. *Clinica Chimica Acta 66:*157.

Sieber, O.F., Jr., and G. Harrison
1979   Pertussis and malnutrition: clinical case. Submitted to *Nutrition Review.*

Sirisinha, S., R. Suskind, R. Edelman, C. Charupatana, and R.E. Olson
1973   Complement and C3-proactivator levels in children with protein-calorie malnutrition and effect of dietary treatment. *Lancet* 1:1016.

Sirisinha, S., R. Suskind, R. Edelman, C. Asvapaka, and R.E. Olson
1975   Secretory and serum IgA in children with protein-calorie malnutrition. *Pediatrics 55:*166.

Smythe, P.M., G.G. Brereton-Stiles, H.J. Grace, A. Mafoyane, M. Schonland, H.M. Coovadia, W.E. Loening, M.A. Parent, and G.H. Vos
1971   Thymolymphatic deficiency and depression of cell mediated immunity in protein-calorie malnutrition. *Lancet 2:*939.

Stare, F.J.
1968   Measles and malnutrition. *Nutrition Review 26:*232.

Suskind, R.M., Editor
1977   *Malnutrition and the Immune Response.* Raven Press, New York.

United States Senate Select Committee on Nutrition and Human Needs
1977   *World Food and Nutrition Study.* U.S. Government Printing Office, Washington, D.C.

Voorhees, M.L., M.J. Stuart, A.J. Stockman, and F.A. Oski
1975   Iron deficiency anemia and increased urinary norepinephrine excretion. *Journal of Pediatrics 63:*54.

Weatherholtz, W.M., T.C. Campbell, and R.E. Webb
1969   Effect of dietary protein levels on the toxicity and metabolism of heptachlor. *Journal of Nutrition 98:*90.

Wiley, B. and N. Maverakis
1968   Virulent and avirulent encapsulated variants of Staphylococcus aureus. *Journal of Bacteriology 95:*998.

Williams, C.D.
1933   *Archives of Diseases of Childhood 8:*423.

Wilson, H.D. and H.F. Eichenwald
1974   Sepsis neonatorum. *Pediatric Clinics of North America 21:*571.

Winick, M.
1976   *Malnutrition and Brain Development.* Oxford University Press, New York.

World Health Organization Study Group
1972   A survey of nutritional-immunological interactions. *Bulletin of the World Health Organization 46:*537.

Malnutrition:
Socio-Economic Effects And Policies
In Developing Countries

Miriam Muñoz de Chavez

In Mexico the term "man of maize" has been coined to describe the type of people raised in a community where the staple foods are tortillas and beans. Their physical development is poor, they are weak and susceptible to diseases, their productive potential is very limited, and their mental and social development is insufficient (Muñoz et al., 1974).

The Mexican National Institute of Nutrition has conducted a series of studies in rural Mexican environments into various factors which go to build the "man of maize." Not only does nutritional insufficiency retard growth and alter body proportions of the growing child, but the mental and social aspects of development are apparently also profoundly affected.

Nutrition and Individual Development

A longitudinal study carried out by A. Chavez and C. Martinez (1973) for the National Institute of Nutrition in the community of Tezonteopan to the south of Mexico City has shown that performance in a number of developmental aspects, including the mental, was deficient among a group of children who received the standard village diet when compared to a paired sample of children who were given a specially supplemented diet. The poor diet was the traditional one of this town, consisting of breast milk, tortillas, and beans, while the supplemented diet consisted of these foods with the addition of cow's milk and other high quality foods. Two children under study are seen in figure 4.1. The taller child is two years younger than the other.

The calorie consumption in the first two years of life of both groups is represented in figure 4.2. This study is unique in that it includes the only longitudinal survey that has been done on consumption of breast milk. This was performed by weighing the children before and after each feeding for a period of 72 hours every two months during the 18 month study. The continuous-line curves indicate the situation of the non-supplemented children, which is the situation of the majority of the mother-child units in the community under study. The mothers secrete enough milk when the infant is born, but at the infant's third month of life the quantity drops to a half a liter a day, a level which then remains constant until almost the end of the lactation period, despite the steadily increasing needs of the growing

Fig. 4.1

infant. Home supplementation to breast feeding is generally provided too late and too little, with timidness, fear, and many prejudices (Chavez, Martinez, and Bourges, 1975).

The differences in total calorie and protein intake between the supplemented and non-supplemented children consumed a total of 450 calories and nine grams of protein — scarcely more than they consumed at the age of three months — but the children in the supplemented project showed a

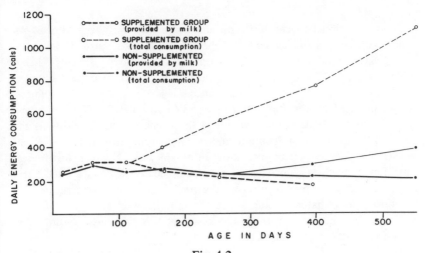

Fig. 4.2

total intake that surpassed 1,000 calories, and their protein intake surpassed 50 grams daily.

There is a Spanish proverb which says, "one can learn to do anything except to go without eating." This is possibly the most mistaken proverb of all. The first thing that the non-supplemented (or "normally raised") children did was to adapt to this low calorie intake. Figure 4.3 shows the differences in the physical activity of these groups of children. At the age of 18 months, children whose diets were supplemented during our program showed six times more activity than the controls. This was measured in a time sampling system, observing each child for ten minutes every hour for a daily 12 hour period (Chavez, Martinez, and Bourges, 1972).

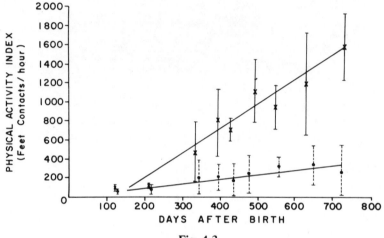

Fig. 4.3

The interaction between nutrition and health has long been known. An undernourished person becomes sick both from lack of nutrients and from the greater tendency to fall victim to infectious diseases. Many epidemiological studies show that malnutrition encourages certain diseases, which, in turn, through metabolic alterations, loss of appetite, and prejudices, favor continued malnutrition (Martinez and Chavez, 1972). The fact is well known that in all developing countries the primary cause of death is the so-called "malnutrition/infection complex." According to studies carried out in rural environments, including those by the Mexican National Institute of Nutrition, possibly as much as 70 percent of deaths of children under five years of age have malnutrition as the underlying cause, complicated by respiratory and diarrheal illnesses as precipitating factors. Some 100,000 children die annually in Mexico as a result of this "malnutrition/infection complex" (Perez Hidalgo and Chavez, n.d.).

To demonstrate the intimate linkage between nutrition and infection, figure 4.4 depicts all the diseases suffered during the first two years of life by

COMPARISON OF DISEASES-A NON SUPPLEMENTED (A) CHILD AND
A SUPPLEMENTED ONE (B)-LONGITUDINAL STUDY

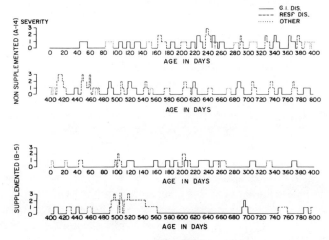

Fig. 4.4

the two children seen in figure 4.1. The entire non-supplemented group
suffered an average of 35 diseases each, mainly respiratory or diarrheal, which
kept them in a condition of illness one third of the time. The supplemental
group not only suffered fewer diseases, 22, but the illnesses were shorter and
less severe.

Figure 4.5 shows the differences between the supplemented experimental

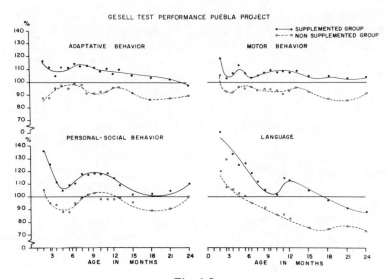

Fig. 4.5

group and the "normal" group regarding mental test performance. Scores were always considerably higher among the supplemented children, especially in adaptive behavior and in language development (Chavez, Martinez, and Yaschine, 1974).

Researchers at the Mexican National Institute of Nutrition also undertook a study of mother-infant interaction, as well as studying the relationship between the child and its environment. It was clearly demonstrated that the malnourished child is more passive, that he interacts very little with his mother, that he sleeps a great deal, and that he demands minimum attention from his family. Consequently, there is very little stimulation to further the child's intellectual and social development. He becomes timid, stays close to his mother, and is very apathetic.

This conduct on the part of malnourished children is expressed in the indigenous Náhuatl language by the word "chipil," which means "jealous." This behavior is attributed in village communities to the psychological effect on the child of the mother's new pregnancy, and not to its real cause: the nutritional insufficiency brought about by the child's removal from maternal breast feeding (Chavez, Martinez, and Yaschine, 1975). It can be inferred that children whose diets were supplemented found their houses too small, as their physical activity was very extensive. Such activity awakened the interest of their parents and of their siblings, thereby establishing a level of interaction among family members never seen before in Tezonteopan. The children's demands grew and the parents were forced to provide very diversified stimuli.

Nutrition and Socio-Economic Development

This study shows the very real importance of nutrition, not only in relation to individual development, but also in relation to social group interaction. The social adaptation of children to malnutrition will undoubtedly continue throughout the rest of their lives, giving rise to little activity, a high degree of dependence, and passivity. Consequently, their participation in the socioeconomic development of the country will be very limited.

It can be stated that the entire developing world — which has as its basic food, in one form or another, a single cereal or a single root — is full of persons with the same nutritionally derived problems. Not only does malnutrition deprive these people of normal social conduct, but it also molds their social station in life. There is no doubt that dependence and passivity by the rural population in the developing world are closely related to malnutrition.

All of this represents a complex problem, in which there are many vicious circles. Production is low because labor and investment are insufficient. This, in turn, is due to deficiencies in the physical and intellectual capabilities of the population, and these deficiencies are the result of dietary insufficiency.

The vicious circle between nutrition and economic development must be broken if the problems confronting the majority of the developing countries are to be solved.

Many points of view have been set forth as to the ultimate cause of malnutrition. Most tend to give major importance to economic factors: poverty, unemployment, and low production. Others consider cultural factors as being the most important. I sincerely believe that, in practice, both these arguments are valid, because all the factors are integral parts of the complex of underdevelopment. However, if I were asked to clarify my position without using the word "underdevelopment," I would point to the social factors outlined in this chapter rather than to these economic or cultural factors.

National Nutrition Policies

During the 1970's several countries have placed emphasis on so-called "national nutrition policies." These nutrition policies are invariably made up of three fundamental components. One is called "vertical integration," which attempts to adjust production to consumption. The second is called "horizontal coordination," which attempts to put into effect a program of stimulating consumption among low income sectors. The third is a series of support programs, which include research and technical support.

In many countries, vertical integration has been achieved through the system known as "food consumption goals." This system consists of planning an adequate availability of basic foods, the correct planning of storage systems, transportation, industrialization, and, finally, bringing influence to bear on commercial systems so as to improve distribution, quality, and food prices.

Vertical integration is easier to achieve in the developed countries, especially in the socialist countries, where central planning systems are quite effective. When this system has been tried in the developing countries, it has met with success, especially over the long run.

Horizontal coordination is extremely important, as nutritional problems are frequently due to deficiencies in food distribution and consumption among sectors, rather than to a real scarcity of food products in a country as a whole. Efforts are made toward food consumption orientation even within the developed countries, but when these efforts are not coordinated, they are simply lost without anything having been achieved. Educational implementation programs, and programs which use the communication media, figure among the most powerful tools of consumer orientation.

Regarding direct nutritional education programs, we should stress the importance of teaching people in poor communities to improve their diets by using those resources which are already available to them locally, and which do not represent any greater expense. As an example, a series of programs were being carried out in Mexico in the 1970's which dealt with education regarding supplementary feeding during the first year of life (Muñoz, 1972).

As has already been mentioned, one of the immediate causes of malnutrition in a rural environment lies in the fact that the production of maternal milk after the infant's third month of life remains at about half a liter a day. In spite of the child's greater need, the mother does not add sufficient supplementary feeding. Mothers in rural areas of Mexico begin to give *atole* (a very thin, watery corn meal mixture) and broths to the infant when it is eight or ten months of age. This problem is more related to cultural factors than to economic ones. That is why an educational solution is called for. This has been demonstrated experimentally in a community where mothers were instructed to make a puree of a mixture of maize and beans to supplement breast feeding. Practically normal growth occurred in these children.

In another experimental study it was possible to demonstrate that, in a rural environment, education through the use of the communication media is also effective. People in rural environments are not constantly exposed to media communication, and their credulity is quite high. It has been observed that both direct and indirect education, at least in the programs which have been studied, have resulted in dramatic improvements in infant nutrition practices, and, to a certain extent, other practices in family nutrition (Muñoz et al., 1975). The greatest effort has been in the provision of milk substitutes and extensors, with the object of ultimately reaching four million milk-deprived children.

Another element which has proved very useful in improving the nutritional status of children in rural Mexico has been the government provision of low-cost, high-nutritive supplements. Lacteous tablets containing protein, some cow's milk, and carbohydrates were manufactured and made available to poor families at very low cost. Also manufactured was a very low-cost extended infant formula type of milk product made up of milk, whey, and carbohydrates. Distribution of this product, however, only occurred in urban areas. Still another product, in powder form, which contains soy beans and 15 percent milk, has reached half a million children a day. In summary, these experiences show the wide range of possibilities afforded by the use of advanced food technology as a means of feeding malnourished people.

These national nutrition policies must be supported by some programs of an economic nature which are designed to increase production in marginal zones, where work and productivity are limited. There should also be certain consumption stimuli among the unemployed population, as well as among the marginal urban population.

The principal obstacle in implementing effective nutrition programs is the lack of socio-political decision-making aimed at satisfying basic requirements of low-income sectors of the population. Public health services have imitated the pattern of the developed countries, which have overcome, by and large, the problems associated with poverty, and therefore give priority to sophisticated medical services. By the late 1970's, many top-level leaders in Mexico became strongly convinced of the necessity for decisive action, and the Mexican government provided the author the opportunity to coordinate the activities of various governmental agencies, with the objective of putting into practice a National Food and Nutrition Policy.

Those involved in nutrition in Mexico are convinced that these programs constitute a very practical technology at relatively low cost. They generate far more resources than they consume, they provide well-being and health, and, above all, they offer to the population the opportunity for individual and social development.

References

Chavez, A., and C. Martinez
1973   Nutrition and development of infants from poor rural areas III: Maternal nutrition and its consequences on fertility. *Nutrition Reports International* 7:1.

Chavez, A., C. Martinez, and H. Bourges
1972   Nutrition and development of children from poor rural areas II: Nutritional level and physical activity. *Nutrition Reports International* 5:139.

Chavez, A., C. Martinez, and H. Bourges
1975   Role of lactation in the nutrition of low socio-economic groups. *Ecology of Food and Nutrition 4:*159.

Chavez, A., C. Martinez, and T. Yaschine
1974   The importance of nutrition and stimuli on child mental and social development. In *Early Malnutrition and Mental Development* XII, Symposium of the Swedish Nutrition Foundation, Almqvist and Wiksell, Uppsala.

Chavez, A., C. Martinez, and T. Yaschine
1975   Nutrition, behavioral development and mother-child interaction in young rural children. Federation of American Societies for Experimental Biology, *Federation Proceedings 34:*1574.

Martinez, C., and A. Chavez
1972   Nutrition and infection in the rural areas. *Summaria, IX Congreso Internacional de Nutricion,* Mexico, D.F., p. 200.

Muñoz, Ch. M.
1972   Searching ways to improving nutrition in less developed areas. *Journal of Nutrition Education 4:*167.

Muñoz, Ch. M., P. Arroyo, S.E. Perez-Gil, M. Hernandez, S.E. Quiroz, M. Rodriquez, P.M. Hermelo, and A. Chavez
1974   The epidemiology of good nutrition in a population with a high prevalence of malnutrition. *Ecology of Food and Nutrition 3:*223.

Muñoz, Ch. M., S.E. Perez-Gil, C. Diez, and J. de Regt
1975   Diffusion of new concepts regarding child nutrition in rural environment. *Ninth Congress on Nutrition,* Karger, Basel, 4:256.

Perez Hidalgo, C., and A. Chavez
n.d.   *Encuestas Nutricionales en Mexico. Volumen III: Estudios en Groupos Especiales.* Ed. Division de Nutricion L-33, Mexico, D.F.

Intersensory Development
In Survivors Of Early Malnutrition
And Stimuli Deprivation

Joaquin Cravioto

In the second half of the twentieth century, health has become a major focus of interest for an increasing number of persons and institutions dealing with social, political, and economic policies. This, in turn, has led to the consideration of nutrition as an important factor in an individual's life from conception on, particularly during the period of growth and maturation. It is generally known that a diet adequate in quantity and quality is vitally important. Nevertheless, Jose Maria Bengoa, in a study of nutritional conditions in twenty-four countries (eight in Africa, twelve in Latin America, and four in Asia) found millions of infants and children affected with moderate or severe forms of malnutrition. Bengoa has also pointed out that, even if at first appearance it is primarily related to environmental and biological factors, nutrition is an integral aspect of the total context of social and cultural factors. At the community level, malnutrition is a man-made disorder, characteristic of the lower economic segments of society, particularly in developing countries where the social system creates malnourished individuals, generation after generation, through a series of social mechanisms. Among these, limited access to goods and services, limited social mobility, and restricted experiential opportunities at crucial points in life play a major role.

Nutritional problems, although affecting the health of large masses of the population, are particularly prevalent in the so-called "vulnerable groups" — small infants and children, and pregnant and lactating mothers — due principally to the sociocultural characteristics of these groups, and to their increased physiological requirements for nutrients.

Data on nutritional deficiency, as well as on low birth weight and prematurity, indicate that deficient nutritional status of the population is perhaps the single most important factor influencing excessive mortality in developing areas. Mothers who have been stunted in their growth by nutritional deficiency in early life have a high frequency of low birth weight infants; many of these infants die from infectious diseases because of their increased vulnerability, while those who survive continue to be at greater risk from the effects of the environment because of nutritional deficiency. It has

[46]

been estimated that in Latin America, for example, the number of deaths resulting directly from malnutrition has been on the order of 50,000 to 60,000 per year. The Inter-American Investigation of Mortality in Childhood, conducted in the 1970's by the Pan-American Health Organization, found that eight percent of all deaths in children six months to two years old had malnutrition as an underlying or main cause, and 41 percent as an associate cause.

The health implications of malnutrition are not confined to mortality and morbidity. Studies in many countries have also shown that survivors of malnutrition exhibit developmental lags not only in psychomotor development but in several other areas, which include hearing and speech, social-personal behavior, problem-solving ability, eye and hand coordination, categorization behavior, intersensory integration, and visual-perceptual competence (Cravioto and De Licardie, 1975). It must be emphasized that the finding of an association between early malnutrition and delayed mental development by no means establishes that insufficient intake of nutrients and calories as such affects intellectual development and learning. Lower socioeconomic status, the risk of malnutrition, and lower mental performance are closely inter-related. Thus, in attempting to test for a relationship between malnutrition and mental development, the research task is to sort out the effect of malnutrition from the effect related to the other variables which may characterize the environment of the malnourished child.

For example, in Mexico, Guatemala, and India (Cravioto and De Licardie, 1973; Cravioto et al., 1967; Srikantia and Sastry, 1972; Cravioto and De Licardie, 1974), studies of families with a very high risk of having severely malnourished children have shown that none of the biological, social, and cultural characteristics of the parents, nor family circumstances (including per capita income, main source of income, and family size) were significantly associated with the presence or absence of severe malnourishment in the child. However, two features of the microenvironment help substantially to identify families with potentially severely malnourished children, long before the appearance of the syndrome. They are a low level of stimulation available in the home, and a passive, traditional mother who is apparently unaware of the needs of her child and responds to him in a minimal way, as if unable to decode the infant's signals. Martínez, Ramos-Galvan, and de la Fuente in Mexico (1951), and Srikantia and Sastry (1972) in India, have also reported a high frequency of severely malnourished children whose mothers exhibit low levels of measured intelligence.

Therefore, our aim should be not only to define malnutrition in terms of the degree of impairment of biological function (physical growth, cognitive development, communicative skills, school performance, resistance to disease, etc.) associated with different degrees of deficit, but also to quantify the synergistic and/or antagonistic effects of the non-nutritional factors (stimuli deprivation, increased morbidity, poor mother-child interaction, etc.). Such factors are almost always present in the lives of malnourished children at different periods of their growth, and with different degrees of deficiency.

It is apparent that testing for the effects of early malnutrition on human mental development can be carried out definitively only by means of a prospective longitudinal study of children at risk, and appropriately selected comparison subjects. Contemporaneously acquired background information for each child, at least from birth onwards, is necessary.

Nutrition and Brain Development: Research Design

A unique opportunity for such a study presented itself in the course of an ecological longitudinal study of growth and development of a total birth cohort born in a preindustrial village in central rural Mexico. Of the 334 children followed from delivery on, 14 girls and eight boys developed severe clinical malnutrition. Age at the time of the diagnoses ranged from four to 53 months, with a single case below one year of age, nine cases between one and two years, eight between two and three years, three between three and four years, and one case diagnosed at 53 months.

Fifteen of the 22 children exhibited kwashiorkor; the other seven cases were marasmus. The proportion of marasmus in females and males was 4:3, while the number of females with kwashiorkor was twice the number of males. These differences are not statistically significant, perhaps due to the small number of cases involved.

Ten children, six with kwashiorkor and four with marasmus, were treated at home, while nine children with kwashiorkor and three with marasmus were treated in a pediatric hospital. No deaths occurred in this latter group, while three of the ten home-treated children died. Of these, two had kwashiorkor and one had marasmus. Ages of these three at the time of diagnosis were 12, 14, and 22 months. In all three children, death occurred within a period of 15 to 60 days after diagnosis.

It seems of interest that these cases occurred despite the fact that all children in the cohort were medically examined on a biweekly basis. Children who failed to grow normally were identified, their infectious illnesses were treated, and their parents were given advice (which they did not follow) on the appropriate feeding and management of children who fail to thrive. In contrast to its lack of influence on the incidence of clinically severe malnutrition, this medical attention decreased the infant mortality rate from a figure of 96 per thousand to 46 per thousand, and reduced the preschool mortality of the cohort by one-half. These data point out once again that traditional medical care can strongly influence mortality while having minimal or no effect on morbidity.

When the research design for the longitudinal study was established, it was decided that a good strategy for the assessment of the possible relation between nutrition and brain development would be to compare the rates of acquisition of certain brain functions between groups with different risks of malnutrition. The level of adequacy in the visual-kinesthetic and in the auditory-visual intersensory modalities was selected as an indicator of brain development. This takes into consideration that the emergence of complex adaptive capacities seems to be underlaid by the growth of increasing liaison and interdependence among the separate sense systems (Birch, 1954; Maier & Schneirla, 1935: Voronim & Guselnikov, 1963), and that the basic mechanism involved in the formation of conditioned responses (i.e., primary learning) is probably the effective establishment and patterning of intersensory organization (Birch & Bitterman, 1949, 1951). Another reason for using intersensory competence as an indicator of neurointegrative development stemmed from the work of Birch and Lefford (1963). They demonstrated that adequacy of intersensory interrelations improves in an age-specific manner, giving developmental curves as regular as those obtained for age and skeletal development.

Visual-Kinesthetic Integration

Visual-kinesthetic competence was explored by a method of equivalence in the perception of geometric forms. The kinesthetic sense modality used was the sensory inputs obtained through passive arm movement. Such motion entails sensory input from the wrist, elbow, and shoulder joints, and from the arm and shoulder muscles, as its principal components. In the test, kinesthetic information is provided by placing the child's preferred arm behind a screen, and, with the arm out of sight, moving it passively through a path tracing a geometric form.

All children were individually examined, with the following explanation given: "In this next game, I am going to show you a shape like this circle. Then I am going to move your hand around like this." The procedure was demonstrated by moving the arm through a triangle, square, and circle. "You are to tell me if the shape your hand moves around is the same as the shape that you see in front of you. To make the game more interesting, I am not going to let you see which shape your hand is going to go around. I will hold your hand behind this screen. You are not to look. We will do it like this." The task was then demonstrated with the hand behind the screen, using a circle as the visual standard test object and the square, triangle, and circle as kinesthetic test objects.

When the examiner was sure that the child had understood the nature of the task, the visual-kinesthetic testing series was begun. The child was asked for a judgment of "same" or "different" for each paired comparison presented. If the subject was doubtful, he was asked to guess. No repetitions of trials were given. No affirmations or corrections were made during the test period.

Judgments were scored as right or wrong. Two kinds of errors were distinguished: an error made when nonidentical forms presented across modalities were judged as being the same, and an error made when identical forms were judged as being different. Only the first kind of error (errors of equivalence) will be discussed here.

Auditory-Visual Integration

The children's ability to integrate auditory and visual stimuli was also individually studied by a method originally developed by Birch and Belmont (1964). The children were asked to identify visual dot patterns corresponding to rhythmic auditory patterns. The task therefore explored the ability to equate a temporally structured set of auditory stimuli with a spatially distributed set of visual ones. Sounds were tapped with a half-second pause between taps for short intervals and a one-second pause for long intervals. The corresponding visual patterns from which the specific selections were to be made were presented immediately after the completion of the auditory stimulation. Each set of visual stimuli was presented on a separate 5 x 8 inch card, and only the specific set of visual dot patterns corresponding to the given auditory presentation was viewed on each trial.

The analysis of these two primary mechanisms underlying cognitive growth focused on a comparison of the levels of performance attained at successive ages by the group of survivors of severe malnutrition, and two groups of children selected from the same birth cohort who were never diagnosed as severely malnourished. One comparison group was matched at birth for sex, gestational age, season of birth, body weight, total body length, and organization of the central nervous system as determined by the Gesell method. The second comparison group included children, full-term and healthy at delivery, who were matched for sex and total scores on home stimulation with the survivors of severe malnutrition. None of the other features of the macroenvironment, including per capita income, main source of income, percentage of total expenditures devoted to food procurement, and family size, nor the biological, educational, and health characteristics of the parents, were different in the three groups of children studied.

Home Stimulation

The instrument used for estimating home stimulation was the inventory developed by Bettye Caldwell (1967), designed to sample certain aspects of the quantity (and in some ways the quality) of social, emotional, and cognitive stimulation available to a young child within his home. Two versions were used, one designed for children up to three years of age, and the other for those three to six years old. In both versions, the selection of items was guided by a set of assumptions about conditions that foster development. Accordingly, the inventory describes and quantifies the following eight areas of the home environment: 1) frequency and stability of adult contact; 2) vocal stimulation; 3) need gratification; 4) emotional climate; 5) avoidance of restriction; 6) breadth of experience; 7) aspects of the physical environment; and 8) available play materials. In each of these areas almost all items receive one of two scores; no attempt is made to rate finer gradations. The total score is the number of items recorded as positive for the child's development. If desired, each area can be scored separately and related to specific features of development.

A trained psychologist recorded the inventory of home stimulation for every child in the cohort at six-month intervals during the first three years of life, and at yearly intervals thereafter. At the time of data collection and scoring, the psychologist was unaware of the nutritional histories of the children.

Study Results

Visual-Kinesthetic Integration

As may be seen in figure 5.1, the mean number of errors in judging non-identical forms presented simultaneously to the visual and kinesthetic sensory modalities decrease as the child matures, both in survivors of severe malnutrition and in controls for size at birth. The patterns of improvement in performance exhibited by both groups approximate the form of a growth function, with a marked difference in the value of the intercept and in the age at which asymptotic values are attained. The control group reaches the asymptote by age 78 months, but it is not yet reached at age 86 months in the survivors of severe malnutrition.

Not only are mean number of errors greater in the survivors, but the variability at all ages studied also is greater. Survivors of malnutrition performed at a significantly lower level of competence at all ages. The data clearly indicate the delay in development of intersensory organization present in these children, right from the first age studied. Thus, at 66 months of age, while seven out of every ten control children did not commit more than 28 errors of equivalence, the corresponding limit for the survivors of malnutrition was 44 errors. At 73 months of age, 75 percent of survivors went down to 48 errors. By contrast, 75 percent of the controls for size at birth reached a figure of no more than 18 errors. The limits of errors for 75 percent of 78-month-old children were 20 and 10, respectively, for survivors and controls. Finally, when the children reached the age of 86 months, 75 percent of the controls had no more than 9 errors, while 75 percent of survivors committed up to 15 errors.

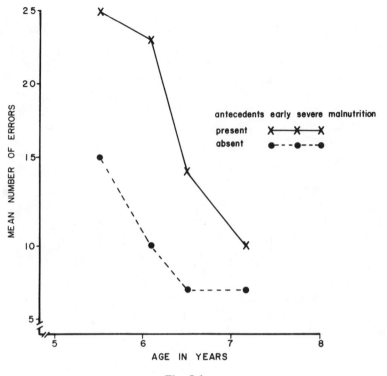

Fig. 5.1

For the development of auditory-visual intersensory integration, the level of competence is markedly inferior for the survivors of severe malnutrition at all ages tested. Starting at age 73 months, it is striking that not a single survivor made at least one correct judgment. On the other hand, the proportion of control children scoring higher than 0 was three out of ten, with one of every ten controls reaching a 5 point score. At 78 months of age, while six out of every ten survivors still had scores of either 0 or 1 correct response, the proportion of so poor performers in the control group was only three out of ten. This same pattern was observed when the children reached 86 months of age (figure 5.2). The proportion of very poor performers—scores of 0 or 1—among the controls was about one-half of the proportion found in the survivors of severe malnutrition. At the other end of the distribution, while not a single survivor gave more than 4 correct judgments, one of every ten control children reached a 6 to 7 level.

The longitudinal data thus clearly show evidence of delayed intersensory integration development in survivors from severe clinical malnutrition.

As was mentioned above, survivors of severe malnutrition and controls

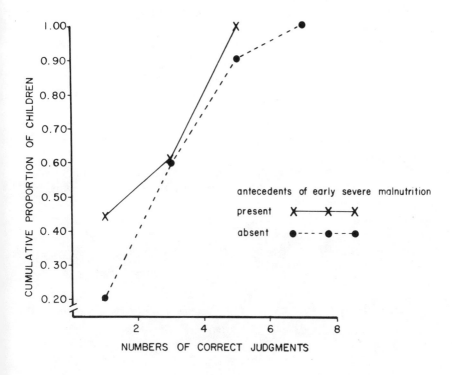

Fig. 5.2

differed not only in the nutritional antecedent, but also in the amount and quality of the stimulation available in their homes. Thus, since on the one hand the antecedent of severe malnutrition was significantly associated with diminished home stimulation, and on the other hand survivors of severe malnutrition showed a significant delay in both kinesthetic-visual and auditory-visual competences, it seemed logical to try to separate the possible effects of the nutritional and the non-nutritional variable. Our attempt to do so was through the inclusion of a control group of children who were never diagnosed as suffering from severe malnutrition, but whose total scores on home stimulation were equal to the scores of the survivors, both before and after the episode of severe clinical malnutrition.

In considering errors it is clear that, for growth functions, the examination of group difference can best be explored after the initial appearance of chance performance and before performance reaches a common maximum level, represented by the asymptote of the growth function. Accordingly, performances at ages 73 and 78 months were selected for analysis of performance on the kinesthetic-visual task, comparing children with and without antecedents of severe clinical malnutrition who were matched for scores on total home stimulation.

Figure 5.3 clearly shows that at 73 months of age, even when matched for home stimulation, survivors of severe malnutrition perform at a much lower level than children without the antecedent of malnutrition. For example, the proportion of control children having 10 or less errors in the judgment of non-identical forms is twice the proportion found in the group of survivors. Similarly, while only two out of every ten controls commit more than 20 errors, the proportion in the survivors rises to five children of every ten exhibiting this low level of competence.

Taking a cut-off point at 25 errors, table 5.1 shows the proportion of children attaining this value. As may be seen, there is a clear gradient of competence among the three groups of children, with the controls for size at birth placed at the highest level, the malnourished at the bottom, and the children matched for home stimulation with the survivors at an intermediate level of competence. A Chi-Square Test of proportions indicates that these figures are significantly different at the 0.05 level of statistical confidence.

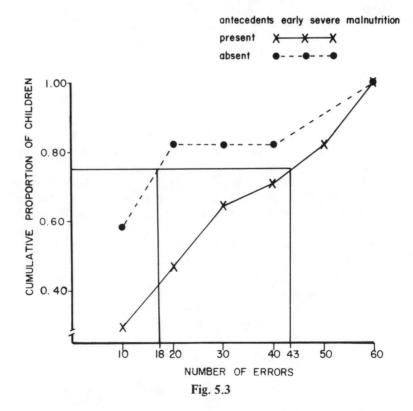

Fig. 5.3

Table 5.1

GROUPS	PROPORTION OF CHILDREN WITH $\lessgtr$ 25 ERRORS.	
MALNOUR	0.529	5 OF 10
SIMSIZE	1.000	10 OF 10
SIMSTIM	0.823	8 OF 10

$$\chi^2 \text{ PROPORTIONS} = 28.87; \quad \text{DF} = 2; \text{ P}<0.05$$
$$(\text{MALNOUR} + \text{SIMSTIM}) \text{ VS. SIMSIZE} = 8.51; \quad \text{DF} = 1; \quad \text{P}<0.05$$
$$\text{MALNOUR VS. SIMSTIM} = 20.36; \quad \text{DF} = 1; \text{ P}<0.05$$

The proportions of 78-month old children with and without antecedents of severe malnutrition, matched for total scores on home stimulation, making different numbers of errors in the kinesthetic-visual task, are presented in figure 5.4. Once again, it is apparent that survivors of severe malnutrition are significantly more advanced in their performance than children with equal scores on stimulation, but without the antecedent of severe malnutrition. At the highest level of performance, i.e., no more than 5 errors, there are twice as many controls as survivors. Similarly, while 75 percent of the controls do not make more than 10 errors, the corresponding figure for survivors is 56 percent.

If one takes a cut-off point at 16 errors, survivors of malnutrition, controls for home stimulation, and controls for size at birth exhibit a gradient of performance in kinesthetic-visual ability similar to that seen for the 73-month old children. Children without antecedents of severe malnutrition and with higher scores on home stimulation placed first, followed by children without antecedents of malnutrition, and, finally, by the survivors of malnutrition, who are the worst performers. Differences among the three groups are statistically significant at the level of confidence of 0.05.

Auditory-Visual Integration

The picture for the development of auditory-visual intersensory integration

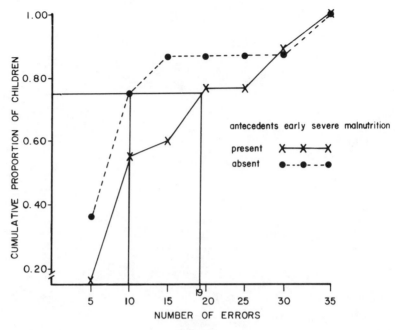

Fig. 5.4

is markedly different than that obtained for the kinesthetic-visual task when survivors of severe malnutrition are compared with children with the same low scores on home stimulation but without the antecedent of malnutrition. With the exception of age 73 months, results do not reach the 5 percent level of statistical significance. In the other two age groups, the proportions of low and high performers are about the same in both groups. At all ages considered, Chi-Square Tests of proportions make evident the lack of difference between children with and without antecedents of severe malnutrition matched for total scores on home stimulation.

Malnutrition and Intersensory Development

Gopalan and his group in India (Champakam et al., 1968; Srikantia et al., 1975), Wray in Thailand (n.d.), and Cravioto and associates in Guatemala and Mexico (1966, 1967, 1970), have published studies on intersensory development in school-age children at risk of having had malnutrition during the preschool age.

In the Indian study, children rehabilitated from kwashiorkor (suffered between the ages of 18 and 36 months) were compared at ages of eight to eleven years with matched controls. Intersensory organization was poorer in the index cases than in the control subjects, with differences highly significant. When these children were again tested five years later, the differences between the two groups had considerably decreased. Although the survivors of severe protein-calorie malnutrition still committed more errors than the control children, the difference was not statistically significant. After another two years, the performance of both groups of children was errorless.

The apparent catch-up of the originally malnourished group has to be considered carefully. When applying a test with a clearly developmental course, the point at which the asymptotic performance is reached might be the only difference between a group with normal development and a group with a developmental delay. If a child has already completed the maximal level of performance, and another child obtains that same level later in time, although both children now have the same score it cannot properly be said that the second child "caught up" with the first. Moreover, in societies where the demands are chronological-age specific, the importance of a delay in development might be fundamental for the future role and status of those affected. This is true in spite of the fact that later in life, such as in adulthood, the test performance of these individuals may not differ at all from that obtained by their more fortunate counterparts.

In the Mexico, Guatemala, and Thailand studies, children aged five through eleven years were tested. According to the physical growth achievement at each age level, the lower quartile of height distribution (most stunted children) and the upper quartile of the distribution (most fully grown children) were contrasted in their intersensory abilities. Differences in neurointegrative skills were manifested in all combinations of intersensory integrations examined. Tall children, particularly in the younger age groups, performed at a higher level of competence than stunted children. Not only were mean differences significant, but individual variability in performance also tended to be greater in the shorter children. Obviously, when height is used as an index of risk of exposure to prior malnutrition, at least three contaminating variables must be controlled in interpreting its association with levels of performance. The first is that height differences should not merely be the reflection of familial differences in stature; the second, that short stature should not be just another manifestation of a general developmental delay; and third, that shorter children must not come from familial environments at significantly lower socio-cultural levels.

These non-nutritional factors were ruled out as main contributors to the results obtained, since: 1) height of parents and children were not significantly correlated; 2) no significant association was found between the height of the fathers and the level of intersensory competence achieved by the child; 3) tall and short children of the same age in populations of children without antecedent conditions of nutritional risk did not exhibit differences in their levels of intersensory adequacy; and, 4) by the lack of correlation between height and income, occupation, housing, personal cleanliness, presence of sanitary facilities in the home, and contact of parents with mass communication media.

Educational level could not be eliminated as an important intervening variable, since the mother's level of formal education was significantly associated with her child's height. Accordingly, the results from Guatemala, Mexico, and Thailand could be interpreted as indicating that the inadequacy in intersensory development could represent the effects of earlier malnutrition, in association with more general subcultural differences between the tall and short children.

The data of the previous studies on kinesthetic-visual intersensory integration are thus in agreement with our data from the longitudinal study, in the sense that the antecedent of severe malnutrition, independently of the characteristics of the stimulation available at home, is *per se* strongly associated with the levels of competence in the kinesthetic-visual task. Since the quality and quantity of the stimulation available at home also showed a significant correlation with the intersensory task, the developmental lag observed in survivors of malnutrition appears to be the result of the effects of earlier malnutrition in association with certain microenvironmental factors related to child care.

The findings in relation to auditory-visual integration give a totally different picture. When the difference in home stimulation between survivors of severe malnutrition and control children was cancelled out, the performance of the survivors was at the same level observed in control children with low scores in stimulation. The disappearance of the developmental lag in the survivors points to a strong association between stimulation available in the home and competence in auditory-visual integration, and to a lack of association between a previous history of severe malnutrition and auditory-visual competence.

Effects of Social Environment

In the attempt to assess the influences of social environment separately from those which may derive from malnutrition as such, studies on children from middle or high socioeconomic classes who suffered secondary malnutrition due to congenital pyloric stenosis or cystic fibrosis seem relevant.

General intelligence assessed by means of the Peabody Picture Vocabulary Test and the Raven Progressive Matrices Test was obtained for 50 children, 44 boys and six girls, aged from five to 14 years, who had been treated for congenital pyloric stenosis. This disease involves a brief period of minimal to gross starvation whose onset ranges from birth to three months of life. Almost immediately after surgical correction, the child is able to consume an adequate diet in sufficient quantity, with rapid recovery of a normal nutritional status. The severity of starvation was determined as a percentage difference between the infant's weight on admission to the hospital and the expected weight for age, extrapolated from weight at birth. Two groups of children were used for comparison. The first was made up of 44 siblings closest in age to the patient. The second control group had 50 children matched, case by case, with the index children for age, sex, and father's level of education. These 50 children were selected as a sub-sample from a random sample representing the population of the county in which the index case children lived (Klein et al., 1975).

Although there was a negative significant intragroup correlation between degree of severity of starvation and measured intelligence ($r=-0.323$; p less than 0.05), and also a significant correlation between severity of starvation and the scores on a scale that measured the parental evaluation of the child's intellectual development and expected educational potential ($r=-.367$; df=49; p less than 0.01), there were not consistent differences in global intelligence among the index cases, siblings, and matched controls.

Berlund and Rabo (1973) studied a group of Swedish adults who had suffered from inanition starting between the ages of six to 20 days due to pyloric stenosis, and found a significant correlation between the height attained at adulthood and the weight loss and duration of the episode of starvation. Nonetheless, performance on an intelligence test administered at the time of military service did not correlate with the antecedent of severe malnutrition in early infancy.

Research by Lloyd-Still et al. (1974) was conducted on intellectual performance, sensory-motor abilities, and social adaptation in a group of 41 patients, aged two to 21 years of age, who had suffered from severe malnutrition in the first six months of life. Thirty-four had cystic fibrosis, three ileal atresia, and the other four had protracted diarrhea. No evidence of socioeconomic deprivation was found. When tested for intellectual performance at the ages of 18 to 72 months, the results on the Merrill Palmer Test were significantly lower in the patients than in a group of siblings of similar age. In the older patients, five years or older, mean IQ values on the WISC or WAIS were not significantly different between index cases and siblings. Neither motor abilities nor social adaptation, measured by the Lincoln-Oseretzky Test and the Vineland Scale respectively, gave significantly different values in patients and siblings.

It seems apparent that non-nutritional factors characteristic of the poor microenvironment of the potentially malnourished child are in themselves capable of influencing mental growth and development. On the other hand, malnutrition *per se* also seems to play a role in development. Thus, in a study on the relation of malnutrition and language development in a cohort of children followed from birth on, in an attempt to separate the possible influences of stimuli deprivation from those of chronic protein-calorie malnutrition of enough severity to depress gain in total body length, an analysis of the interrelations among these two variables and the number of bipolar concepts present at 46 months of age was carried out. A technique of partial correlation was used in order to estimate the degree of association between two of the variables, holding constant the effect of the third variable. When the relation between body height and number of bipolar concepts was partialed out for home stimulation, the coefficient of correlation changed from 0.26 to 0.23, keeping its statistical significance at the 0.05 level of confidence.

This finding suggests that the association of height, as an indicator of nutritional status, and number of bipolar concepts is to a large extent independent of the effect of home stimulation. When the relation between home stimulation and number of bipolar concepts was partialed out for body height, the coefficient of correlation dropped from 0.20 to 0.15, and when the number of bipolar concepts was held constant, the coefficient of correlation between home stimulation and body height changed from 0.23 to 0.19. These results could be interpreted to mean that home stimulation contributes relatively more to body height than to number of bipolar concepts, while body height contributes more than home stimulation to the variance in bipolar concepts (Cravioto and De Licardie, 1975).

In children rehabilitated from malnutrition, Klein et al. (1972) have reported that the level of prediction of cognitive function given by sociocultural factors (such as quality of dwelling, father's formal education, mother's dress, mother's personal cleanliness, task instruction, and social contacts) is significantly increased with the inclusion of body height and head circumference. Similarly, Richardson (1976) found that the IQs of Jamaican school age children who had suffered severe protein-calorie malnutrition in infancy were correlated with the presence of the episode of severe malnutrition as such, with total body length at the time of intelligence testing, and with a measure of the child's social background. The percentage of explained variance was greatest for the social attribute and lowest for the episode of malnutrition; body height gave an intermediate value.

As a part of their longitudinal study on growth and development, De Licardie and Cravioto (1974) decided to analyze the behavioral styles of response of children with and without a documented episode of severe clinical malnutrition. In order to control for level of measured intelligence, a comparison group of children of the same sex and IQ as the survivors of malnutrition was included, besides a group of children without antecedents of severe malnutrition whose body weight, height, and head, chest, and arm circumferences at birth were equal to those of the malnourished children. Significant differences were found between the styles of response according to the presence or absence of antecedent severe malnutrition. Differences in IQ could not account for differences in the style with which the child approached the task given by the examiner. The survivors of malnutrition differed from the control children in the amount and type of stimulation available in their homes. In trying to separate out the effects of stimuli deprivation from those that might be ascribed to early malnutrition, survivors and controls with equal scores in home stimulation were identified. When the styles of response of these children were compared, controls matched at birth expressed their verbal "not-work" responses in terms of rationalizations of competence. Survivors of severe malnutrition expressed their responses predominantly as requests for aid, and controls matched for sex and IQ with the survivors had similar proportions of styles of competence, requests for aid, and substitution of the task. These findings seem to indicate that, besides the effect of stimuli deprivation on the style of response, the antecedent of severe malnutrition appears to be another modulator of the style of behavior.

Integrative Effect of Nutrition and Stimulation

Experimental research on animals also leads to a consideration of an integrative effect of nutrition and stimulation. In this respect, Castilla et al. (1973) reported the synergistic effects of malnutrition and stimuli deprivation on the biochemical structure of the brain, confirming and extending to another experimental model the findings of Levistky and Barnes (1972) on the effects of nutrition and isolation on animal behavior. Barnes and his associates, on the basis of their results from a large series of animal experiments (Barnes, 1968; Frankova and Barnes, 1968; Barnes et al., 1970; Levistky and Barnes, n.d.; Barnes, 1976), prefer to speak of the interaction between malnutrition and environmental stimulation. The similarity of the biochemical changes produced in the brain by nutrition or by stimulation have led them to consider that the physiological mechanisms which may be responsible for the long-term beneficial effects of early stimulation may not be operative if a concurrent state of malnutrition is present during a critical period of development.

Malnutrition may thus change the experience of perception of the environment by physiologically rendering the animal less capable of receiving or integrating (or both) information about the environment. These authors have also considered that even in the absence of biochemical alterations of the brain, malnutrition may elicit behavior that is incompatible with the incorporation of environmental information necessary for optimum cognitive development. Behavior primarily food-oriented and behavior expressed as apathy and social withdrawal are two examples of the kind of behaviors exhibited with a very high frequency by survivors of early malnutrition.

It is fortunate that the study of malnutrition as a possible cause of sub-optimal mental development in human children has gone beyond the simplistic attempt to consider the nutritional factor as the sole cause of the lower performance and distorted behavior observed in survivors of malnutrition.

Since early development is characterized by the changing nature and organization of mental abilities, and the notion of a unitary intelligence factor may not be meaningful until age five (Bayley, 1958; Bloom, 1964; McCall et al., 1972), it could be speculated that, among the specific mental abilities, some might be influenced by certain specific environmental or host factors, while other abilities would be influenced by other specific factors. This speculation seems to be in accordance with findings that suggest that early performance in tests of specific abilities may be better predictors of IQ at later ages than tests that are aggregates of various specific abilities. Along this same line would be the reports showing better prediction of mental performance in early infancy by socioeconomic indicators than by mental scales (Broman et al., 1975), and the studies of Pedersen and Wender (1968), who found significant associations between early social behavior and certain forms of cognitive and perceptual abilities. For example, they found children who at two and one-half years of age were categorized as more contact-oriented and showed more attention-seeking behavior, and who had significantly lower nonverbal intellectual functioning four years later.

The importance of sorting out specific mental abilities as a function of macro and micro environmental factors that would exert a more powerful influence on them is obvious from both practical and theoretical viewpoints. It is of primary importance to recognize, as did John Dobbing (1976), that perhaps no single disadvantage plays a major part in lowering human achievement. It is hoped that humans may have a great capacity to compensate for one disadvantage by an advantage in another direction.

References

Barnes, R.H.
1968   Behavioral changes caused by malnutrition in the rat and pig. In *Environmental Influences,* D.C. Glass, ed., Rockefeller University Press and Russell Sage Foundation, New York, p. 52.

Barnes, R.H.
1976   Dual role of environmental deprivation and malnutrition in retarding intellectual development. *American Journal of Clinical Nutrition 29:*912.

Barnes, R.H., A.V. Moore, and W.G. Pond
1970   Behavioral abnormalities in young adult pigs caused by malnutrition in early life. *Journal of Nutrition 100:*145.

Bayley, N.
1958   Value and limitation of infant testing. *Children 5:*129.

Berlund, G., and E. Rabo
1973   A long-term follow-up investigation of patients with hypertrophic pyloric stenosis – with special reference to the physical and mental development. *Acta Paediatrica Scandinavica 62:*125.

Birch, H.G.
1954   Comparative Psychology. In *Areas of Psychology,* F. Marcuse, ed., Harper, New York, p. 446.

Birch, H.G., and L. Belmont
1964   Auditory-visual integration in normal and retarded readers. *American Journal of Orthopsychiatry 34:*852.

Birch, H.G., and M.E. Bitterman
1949   Reinforcement and learning: the process of sensory integration. *Psychological Review 56:*292.

Birch, H.G., and M.E. Bitterman
1951   Sensory integration and cognitive theory. *Psychological Review 58:* 335.

Birch, H.G., and A. Lefford
1963   *Intersensory Development in Children.* Monographs of the Society for Research in Child Development, Serial 89, Vol. *28*(5):1.

Bloom, B.S.
1964   *Stability and Change in Human Characteristics.* John Wiley and Sons, New York.

Broman, S.H., P.L. Nichols, and W.A. Kennedy
1975   *Preschool I.Q.: Prenatal and Early Development Correlates.* John Wiley and Sons, New York.

Caldwell, B.M.
1967   Descriptive evaluations of child development and of development settings. *Pediatrics 40:*46.

Castilla, S.L., A.Q. Cravioto, and J. Cravioto
1973   Efecto de la estimulacion y nutricion a temprana endad sobre el desarrollo bioquimico del sistema nervioso central. 1-hallazgos durante el periodo de desnutricion cronica. Mexican Society for Pediatric Research Meeting, San Jose Vista Hermosa, Mexico, December 1973.

Champakan, S., S.G. Srikantia, and C. Gopalan
1968   Kwashiorkor and mental development. *American Journal of Clinical Nutrition 21:*884.

Cravioto, J., H.G. Birch, and E.R. De Licardie
1967   Influencia de la desnutricion sobre la capacidad de aprendizaje del nino escolar. *Boletin Medico Hospital Infantil de Mexico 24:*217.

Cravioto, J., H.G. Birch, E.R. De Licardie, and L. Rosales
1967   The ecology of infant weight gain in a preindustrial society. *Acta Paediatrica Scandinavica 56:*71.

Cravioto, J., and E.R. De Licardie
1970   Mental performance in school age children. Findings after recovery from early severe malnutrition. *American Journal of Diseases of Children 120:*404.

Cravioto, J. and E.R. De Licardie
1973   Environmental correlates of severe clinical malnutrition and language development in survivors from kwashiorkor or marasmus. *Panamerican Health Organization Bulletin* (English Edition) 7:50.

Cravioto, J., and E.R. De Licardie
1974   Mother-infant relationship prior to the development of clinical severe malnutrition in the child. *Proceedings of the IV-Western Hemisphere Nutrition Congress,* Bal Harbour, Florida, August, 1974; p. 126.

Cravioto, J. and E.R. De Licardie
1975   Malnutrition chez l'enfant. Les repercussions sur l'individu et la collectivite. *Revue Tiers Monde, t. XVI,* (No. 63):525.

Cravioto, J., E.R. De Licardie, and H.G. Birch
1966   Nutrition growth and intersensory development: An experimental and ecologic study. *Pediatrics 38:*319.

64 JOAQUIN CRAVIOTO

De Licardie, E.R., and J. Cravioto
1974   Behavioral responsiveness of survivors of clinically severe malnutrition to cognitive demands. In *Early Malnutrition and Mental Development,* Cravioto, J., L. Hambraeus, and B. Valhquist, eds., Almqvist and Wiksell, Uppsala, Sweden, p. 134.

Dobbing, J.
1976   Vulnerable periods in brain growth and somatic growth. In *The Biology of Human Fetal Growth,* Roberts, D.F., and Thomson, A.M. eds, Taylor and Francis, London, p. 137.

Frankova, S., and R.H. Barnes
1968   Effect of malnutrition in early life on avoidance conditioning and behavior of adult rats. *Journal of Nutrition 96:*485.

Klein, P.S., G.B. Forbes, and P.R. Nader
1975   Effects of starvation in infancy (pyloric stenosis) on subsequent learning abilities. *Pediatrics 87:*8.

Klein, R.E., B.M. Lester, C. Yarbrough, and J.P. Habitch
1972   *On Malnutrition and Development: Some Preliminary Findings.* Proceedings of the First International Congress of Nutrition, Mexico.

Levistky, D.V., and R.H. Barnes
1972   Nutritional and environmental interactions in the behavior development of the rat: Long-term effects. *Science 176:*68.

Levistky, D.V., and R.H. Barnes
n.d.   Malnutrition and animal behavior. In *Nutrition, Development and Social Behavior,* Kallen, D.J. ed., USGPO, Publication No. NIH73-242, Washington, D.C.

Lloyd-Still, J.D., I. Hurwitz, P.H. Wolff, and H. Schwachman
1974   Intellectual development after malnutrition in infancy. *Pediatrics 54:*306.

Maier, N.R.F., and T.C. Schneirla
1935   *Principles of Animal Behavior.* McGraw-Hill, New York.

Martinez, P.D., R. Ramos-Galvan, and R. De La Fuente
1951   Los factores ambientales en la pelagra de los ninos en Mexico. *Boletin Medico del Hospital Infantil de Mexico.*

McCall, R.B., P.S. Hogarty, and N. Hulburt
1972   Transitions in infant sensorymotor development and the prediction of childhood I.Q. *Psychologist 27:*728.

Pendersen, F.A., and P.H. Wender
1968   Early social correlates of cognitive functioning in six-year old boys. *Child Development 39:*185.

Richardson, S.A.
1976   The relation of severe malnutrition in infancy to the intelligence of school children with differing life histories. *Pediatric Research 10:*57.

Srikantia, S.G., and C.Y. Sastry
1972   Effect of maternal attributes on malnutrition in children. In *Proceedings of the First Asian Congress of Nutrition,* India, p. 584.

Srikantia, S.G., C.Y. Sastry, and A.N. Naidu
1975   *Malnutrition and Mental Function.* Proceedings of the Tenth International Congress of Nutrition, Kyoto, Japan, August 3-9.

Voronin, L.G., and V. Guselnikov
1963   On the phylogenesis of internal mechanisms of the analytic and synthetic activity of the brain. *Pavlov Journal of Higher Nervous Activity 13:*193.

Wray, J.
n.d.   Intersensory Development of School Age Children at a High Risk of Malnutrition During their Preschool Years. Unpublished Manuscript.

The Fortification of Foods

Stanley N. Gershoff

We really do not know as much about nutrition as we think we do. To many people, nutrient fortification or enrichment is attractive as a major weapon in the war against malnutrition because it provides a simple way of increasing the nutrient content of foods. In an ideal program, basic characteristics of the supplemented foods, such as taste, odor, and appearance, should not be altered, and therefore educational programs or changes in eating customs should not be necessary. But is fortification really effective?

In 1968, the U.S. Agency for International Development (AID) funded three major amino acid fortification studies (U.S.A.I.D., 1976). The author directed a rice fortification study in Thailand, another study was conducted in Tunisia on wheat, and a third on corn in Guatemala. All three studies yielded essentially the same results: no measurable health benefits resulted from fortification. Since all of the studies were conducted properly, these results have been disturbing.

The development of low cost, practicable programs to improve the health of people in these and other countries is urgently needed, and it will thus be important to determine why this fortification was ineffective. Nutritional causes of retarded growth and development in the children of the countries studied were poorly understood. In the Thai study, an area was picked where food shortage was not a problem. Furthermore, morbidity studies which were conducted on all subjects every 15 days for three years indicated that growth retardation was not due to disease. Similarly, in Guatemala, there was no food shortage in the area studied. A review of the three studies indicates that a likely reason for the lack of fortification effectiveness has been the low calorie density of the diets consumed. It has been suggested that children were unable to consume enough food to meet their calorie needs, even though food supplies were ample. However, this is conjecture. To those of us interested in establishing effective low-cost nutrition programs in developing countries, much time has been lost. If fortification is to be of value, more information will be needed.

Evaluating Effectiveness

Is there any evidence that large scale fortification programs have had a major beneficial effect on the health of people? I believe that the answer is yes, although the data are very disappointing and hard to evaluate. In the U.S., for example, we have been fortifying foods since about 1940. It is common to add thiamin, riboflavin, niacin, and iron to such foods as bread and pasta. These nutrients and others are added to cornmeal, corn grits, white rice, and processed cereals. Vitamin D is added to fluid milk, skim milk, and non-fat dry milk; vitamin A is also added to fluid and dry milk and to margarine. Iodine is added to table salt. Flouride is added to water in many parts of the country. A large number of foods, particularly artificial beverages, have been fortified with vitamin C. We have essentially overcome the problem of vitamin deficiencies in the U.S. The question is: has this been a result of fortification, or, rather, of improved overall nutrition resulting from the enormous increase in the standard of living? There is clear evidence that iodine fortification eliminated goiter, and that vitamin D fortification has had a real effect on the incidence of rickets, although many people might argue that the decrease in rickets in the U.S. and Western Europe is, in great part, a result of improved pediatric care.

A good example of the sort of problems encountered in evaluating fortification programs can be derived from experiences in Newfoundland (Anon., 1949). In 1944, a nutrition survey in Newfoundland indicated that the population had major nutrition problems. People exhibited a variety of clinical and biochemical signs of chronic nutrient deficiencies. A variety of measures were instituted to improve the situation, including educational campaigns, free distribution of milk powder and cod liver oil to many schools, and distribution of orange juice to expectant and nursing mothers. All margarines were fortified with vitamins. Four years later, a second survey was undertaken. The nutritional status of the population had improved markedly, as demonstrated by clinical and biochemical assessments. The question which could not be answered was: "How much of the improvement was due to nutritional interventions?" There had been a concomitant marked increase in income, accompanied by a doubling of imports of fresh fruit, juices, and vegetables, and increases in the consumption of eggs, fats and oils, green leafy vegetables, and fish and meat.

One often hears about the need for evaluating programs; these evaluations are very difficult to make, whether they concern fortification programs, food stamp programs, the school lunch program, the WIC program, or any of many other programs that have been advocated and developed both in the U.S. and abroad. Nevertheless, I believe that the potential for fortification as a significant method for attacking malnutrition remains attractive.

Fortification Standards

However, considerable understanding of the nature of fortificants and carrier foods, and of the dynamics of fortification programs, is still needed. In

1968 the Council on Food and Nutrition of the American Medical Association, and the Food and Nutrition Board of the National Research Council, recommended fortification of foods under the following conditions (Anon., 1968): 1) the intake of the nutrients to be added is below the desired level in the diets of a significant number of people; 2) the food is likely to be consumed in quantities which make a significant dietary contribution to the population; 3) the nutrient's addition would not be likely to create an imbalance of essential nutrients; 4) the nutrient is stable under proper conditions of storage and use; 5) the nutrient added is physiologically available; and 6) there is a reasonable assurance against excessive intake to a level of toxicity.

To meet such standards in designing a fortification program, it would be necessary to find ways to determine what a "significant number" of people is, and also whether or not these people are receiving the desired amount of one or more of the nutrients. Grain and dairy products are often the vehicle for fortification programs because they are likely to be consumed in significant quantities. A look at nutrition survey data in which the intake of nutrients is compared to income indicates that there are few significant variations which income in the intakes of thiamin, niacin, and riboflavin, vitamins which are added to wheat and other grain products, while for nutrients such as calcium and vitamin C, which are found mainly in more expensive foods, there is a marked decrease in intake as income drops.

The prevailing conditions of food preparation and storage in many areas of the world where nutrient fortification might be of value are far from ideal, so a detailed knowledge of the range of stability of any fortificant is important. Iron fortification in the U.S. represents unsuccessful fortification because most of the iron added to our foods is in a form which is not physiologically available. Again, greater understanding of the characteristics of fortificants is needed.

Finally, in contrast to the developing countries, the U.S. embarked on a "vitamin race" in the 1970's. A cereal such as *Total* contains 100 percent of the adult RDA for a variety of nutrients in an amount of cereal representing about 2½ percent of the daily calorie need of a not very active adult. If all foods were manufactured in this way, we would eat about 40 times the RDA for many essential nutrients, which would not be beneficial, and might even be dangerous. Thus, careful control in fortification programs is necessary.

Carrier Characteristics

A variety of foods can be used as carriers for additional nutrients. Berg and Levinson have written extensively on the characteristics of carriers and on problems in the implementation of fortification programs (Berg and Levinson, 1969; Berg, 1973). They have pointed out that a fortification carrier should have the following characteristics: 1) it should be consumed by a sizeable portion of the public; 2) it should be of such a nature that when it is processed at home the fortificant is not lost; 3) it should be consumed in relatively constant amounts through the year; 4) it should be inexpensive enough so that those people who need it can buy it; and 5) it should be processed in amounts large enough to permit control of the fortification. This last point was a major problem for us in the fortification of rice in Thailand, where every village has one or two small mills. In India there are over half a million rice mills. These situations differ from that which we observed in Tunisia, where most of the wheat flour was processed in a small number of large mills and fortificants could easily be added.

Another characteristic of the carrier is that it should be of such a nature that the fortificant will not alter its taste, odor, or appearance, at least to the point where it affects consumer acceptance. This turns out to be quite a problem. Riboflavin, for example, is a brilliant yellow, and the fortification of rice with riboflavin changes the color of the rice. For many years, it was very difficult to fortify rice with riboflavin in places like Taiwan and Japan, even though a 1955 survey of the Taiwanese army indicated that 90 percent of the soldiers exhibited mouth lesions characteristic of riboflavin deficiency. Today, after many years of nutrition education, yellow rice is prestigious in both of these countries. In our work in Thailand, we had trouble with thiamin, which has an unpleasant odor. When we put it in the rice of people who get 70 to 80 percent of their calories from rice (and are thus very sensitive to its taste and smell), they complained. There are similar problems with iodine. In a study of 52 American companies which provide T.V. dinners and other kinds of convenience foods, only two of them used iodized salt.

Also, the carrier must not alter the stability of the fortificant. An attempt to use salt as a carrier for lysine resulted in a dark salt with a pungent odor.

Another important consideration is that fortification should not significantly alter food economics. The addition of calcium to salt, as suggested in India and Egypt, might actually make it less expensive, since calcium carbonate is a little less costly than sodium chloride, while the addition of iron to salt in India was estimated a few years ago to increase its cost by about 10 percent. Fortification of salt with lysine, which has been suggested, even if it were otherwise feasible, would increase the cost of salt prohibitively.

Planning Fortification Programs

If carriers that have all the desirable characteristics are available, and it is decided as a result of controlled field studies that needed health benefits in developing countries can be realized by using fortified food, a whole new series of questions arises, as discussed by Berg and Levinson (1969). Should the fortification be mandatory by government decree, or should it be voluntary? If it is decided that it should be voluntary, how should the fortified food be distinguished from the non-fortified food? This would be a particularly important problem if the fortification did not change the color, taste, and odor of the food.

Problems of setting and enforcing standards for the nutritional quality and purity of the fortificants are not only problems for developing countries, but also for developed ones. When the U.S. decided to allow 30 percent texturized soy protein into the school lunch program as a substitute for other protein-containing foods, many nutritionists became concerned. Not only was the biological value of the soy protein questionable, but the texturized protein did not contain the non-protein nutrients which had been found in the foods being replaced.

Should the cost of fortification be passed on to the consumer or should it be subsidized by the government? Should subsidies make fortified food less expensive than unfortified food? It has been suggested that if the cost of 100 pounds of salt in Thailand, for example, was increased by one cent because it was iodized, nobody would buy it. Alternatively, one could suggest that it be subsidized, so that it would cost a cent less. It is clear that many of the problems of implementing fortification or other nutrition programs are economic, particularly in those countries which need them the most because of the poverty of their people. Decisions to develop fortification programs often signify the spending of hard currency on imported nutrients and fortification equipment. Fortification programs, particularly those involving amino acids, can appear inexpensive or costly depending on one's point of view. A lysine fortification program for India estimated to "only" cost $1/person/year would also cost about half a billion dollars.

Relatively simple methods for attacking complex health problems are attractive. For many nutritionists, and for AID's Office of Nutrition, the fortification of cereal grains in developing countries around the world had great appeal as a universal remedy in the late 1960's. Over 30 nutrition surveys by the Interdepartmental Committee for Nutrition for National Defense had been completed in developing countries all over the world. An enormous amount of data had been collected in these and other countries with the result that many nutritionists thought they fully understood the complexity of nutrition problems. In most developing countries, 70 percent (plus or minus 10 percent) of the calorie intake comes from either corn, wheat, or rice. A technology appeared to exist for fortifying these grains with needed nutrients, and pressure was applied to institute national programs rather than undertake more "studies."

It is felt by many that when health planners advocate expensive programs, they have an obligation to test them so that political and administrative decision-makers can estimate what they can reasonably expect for their money. This is particularly important in developing countries, which have limited economic resources. In any event, findings have indicated that · large-scale public health nutrition programs should not be initiated without more convincing field study evidence that they will be effective. A greater understanding of the many factors involved in adding fortification to foods is obviously needed before it can be fully relied upon as another weapon in the war against malnutrition.

References

Anonymous
   1949   Resurvey of nutrition in Newfoundland. *Nutrition Revues 7:*331.
Anonymous
   1968   Improvement of nutritive quality of foods. *Journal of the American Medical Association 205:*868.

Berg, A.
   1973   *The Nutrition Factor.* The Brookings Institution, Washington, D.C.

Berg, A. D. and F. J. Levinson
   1969   A new need: the nutrition programmer. *American Journal of Clinical Nutrition 22:*893.

United States Agency for International Development
   1976   Improving the Nutrient Quality of Cereals II. U.S. Government Printing Office, Washington, D.C.

The Food And People Dilemma

Georg Borgstrom

People in the United States have a very vague notion of the nature and magnitude of the world food crisis. Misconceptions regarding the world food and population picture are commonly conveyed by the U.S. educational system at all levels. Important historical and biological factors must be seen in proper perspective in order to provide a desperately needed understanding of the true implications of what is unfolding.

When Europe reached its maximum food production capacity, its people staged the biggest migration in history, siphoning off one-fourth of its population between 1850 and 1950. For two centuries, Europe had been steadily lifting its food ceiling through agricultural advances. But toward the middle of the 1800's the population reached a critical level in relation to food resources. Poverty, unemployment, and hunger rose despite industrialization.

Europeans then rapidly populated the Western Hemisphere, as well as parts of Africa, Oceania, and Siberia. By this international transcendence of their confinement, they lost their awareness of the limitations of our planet. They laid hands on vast grass and forest lands, which doubled their tilled acreage and tripled their pastures.

This grand happening must be seen in the perspective of mankind's lengthy history. Several other regions of the world have previously been populated to capacity. China's population reached the size of the twentieth century United States, exceeding 200 million, around 1670, and by the 1970's had quadrupled to 800 million. India's population reached 200 million in 1860 and had tripled by the 1970's to 600 million.

In both instances, the ecological balance was devastated through the sequence of deforestation, flooding, soil erosion, and siltation. The agricultural repercussions of this are still felt, and were presumably brought under control in China only in the 1970's. The deforestation of the Middle East and the Mediterranean area, which reached its height about 2,000 years ago, resulted in much topsoil being carried to the Mediterranean Basin, with consequent desertification. Tillage in Europe reached highest up the hillsides in the century between 1350 and 1450, never to return as the topsoil was forever lost. The migrants took little lesson from this, and, in taking over North America, repeated the destruction of forestlands and soils.

There were two dramatic consequences of the European migration to new lands. This was the first time hunger disappeared from the Western scene.

[71]

During this 1850-1950 period, transcontinental railroads and transoceanic shipping emerged and made possible for the first time long-distance hauling of food and animal feed. All of this laid the foundation for the world trade pattern which remained dominant until the 1970's, when it was first challenged.

Acreage and Trade

Few Americans seem to realize the perspective of extreme advantage from which they observe the rest of the world. Three times more tilled land is used to feed each American (1.5 acres) than in the developing world; in addition 3.5 acres of pastureland are used for each American. Besides, Americans live under such favorable climatic conditions that as much as 21 percent of the U.S. land area can be tilled. This is twice the global average of 10.5 percent. People in the U.S. hold 13 percent of the world's tilled land, but constitute merely 5.2 percent of the world's population. This explains why they can use about one-third of this great soil asset for world market sales. It also accounts for the fact that, together with still more fortunate Canada, the U.S. makes almost nine-tenths of the net grain deliveries to the world's households. It carries, in such terms, a far greater relative world responsibility than the Middle East does with oil.

The big U.S. grain export has led to the false notion that it is feeding the world. This overlooks the fact that trade never accounted for more than one-tenth of what mankind is eating. But more important is the fact that half of the U.S. cereal export is used to feed livestock. To this must be added its soybean export, which also moves to support the protein sanctuaries of the developed world. In the public mind, and even in that of many knowledgeable circles, trade has become synonymous with aid. The chief recipients of the net trade in cereal grains are, in effect, Europe, Japan, and the Soviet Union. Only in a few years during the 1970's did China and India together receive more grain than Japan. Several European countries have been the recipients of as much or even more grain than either China or India.

The entire debate has been caught in the semantic trap of "grain deficit countries," failing to identify the truly deficient countries which are depending on large additional acreages abroad (ghost acreages), such as Europe (both West and East) and Japan, constituting dominant burdens on the world household. Some European countries have as little land per capita as Asia's teeming millions, but they scan the world and manage via trade and fisheries to depend on big additional acreages. This is rarely ever recognized. Most European countries supplement their acreage, through trade, into the same magnitude as North America, measured per person.

China and India figure at the bottom of the list in grain imports with some 6 to 7 kilograms per capita. Their ghost acreage is almost nil; both sustain a countervailing export of vital agricultural commodities. The West must move out of this outmoded pattern, shaped in the bygone grand period of colonialism.

Colonialism directed towards the warm latitudes resulted in insignificant migration, but it gave rise to a land-demanding plantation economy, the main objective of which was to provide, via trade, the needs of the homelands. During three hundred years of Western colonialism, the world was exploited as one vast warehouse primarily for the benefit of Westerners. In this way, the amount of food available in the colonized regions shrank, often to the serious detriment of the indigenous peoples. This tug of war goes on, and has, in most instances, been critically intensified, as, for example, in West Africa, Central America, and Brazil (where cattle ranches raise beef for export to the U.S.). Japan has created a worldwide network of survival bases in the developing world. Almost the only significant counter-trend has been the development of oilseed crops (sunflower, rapeseed, etc.), so that countries in temperate latitudes are no longer so heavily dependent on oilseed from the poor and hungry countries.

Paradoxically, the U.S. is not only the biggest exporter of food and animal feed, at the rate of more than 22 billion dollars a year; at the same time, it is the world's biggest importer, thereby not only reducing its contribution to the world household but cutting in half agriculture's input into the trade balance. The U.S. is, in effect, the world's largest buyer of beef and of canned meat, as well as of casein.

Europe's net importation amounts to an added tilled acreage of more than 74 million hectares. Japan is depending on a ghost acreage in trade exceeding 3.5 times the tilled land of the homeland. Europe is buying more plant protein per year than the whole Indian subcontinent is eating, and Japan approximately one-third of that. Europe is receiving 28 percent of all cereal grain deliveries to the world market, as well as 84 percent of its oilseed cake and meal, and 68 percent of the protein in soybeans and soybean cake and meal end up in Europe. Europe is further buying almost as much peanut protein from India (chiefly through meal) as from Africa; together, they would suffice to supplement adequately the cereal diet of 165 million people. Japan, with less than five percent of Asia's people, is the recipient of 40 percent of the cereal flow to the continent.

U.S. Agriculture

The U.S. produces about two-thirds of the world soybean crop and has 85 percent of the world export market. This export is frequently touted as a major contribution to alleviating world hunger, but this is highly deceptive since merely a fraction, even on the domestic scene, is channeled into human food. European farmers rely on U.S. soybeans to fatten their poultry, hogs, and cattle. The soybeans exported as beans and meal, with Europe and Japan as chief recipients, carry the potential of supplementing the diet of no less than 1.9 billion cereal eaters. Less than five percent of soybean exports served this purpose in the 1970's.

China has cultivated soybeans for over 4,000 years, and was early forced to use them mainly to feed people. In contrast, the U.S. has grown this crop for less than 60 years and only on scale since the 1950's. In the 1930's soybeans were frequently plowed under for the fertilizing of family farms. Soybeans now joust with corn and wheat as U.S. champion exports, bringing in more foreign exchange than any manufactured items, including jet aircraft and computers.

U.S. agriculture can be highly proud of its accomplishments, but it is not served well by perpetrating the false notion that it is number one in almost all regards. A whole series of fallacies prevail in this respect. The U.S. is top-ranking in yield of corn per acre but does not lead in most other crops. More than 25 countries have a higher wheat yield than the U.S., and among them are countries belonging to the developing world. It is frequently stated that each U.S. farmer feeds 46 to 52 other people. The truth of the matter is that few farmers remain who are capable of feeding themselves (buying key items such as bread, eggs, milk, and others). Behind each farmer stand major subsidiary armies of helpers, indispensable to his operation.

Waste and Utilization

The most neglected aspect of the food issue is what I term the "third dimension," i.e. waste, spoilage, and utilization. Between harvest and consumption, man's competitors in the shape of rodents, birds, insects, and microorganisms take an unreasonable toll of 30 to 50 percent. Measures to reduce these heavy losses could be tied to plans for contingency storage. In addition, considerable losses also occur prior to harvest through pests, weeds, and diseases. The rice yield is cut to less than half in this way.

There are, however, still more insidious losses due to negligence or mismanagement. More than one-fourth of the milk protein produced is allowed to go to waste or to be fed to farm animals. Oilseed protein, in an amount almost four times that of leguminous seeds, is either wasted or used in animal feeds. Only a fraction goes into human food. In U.S. shrimping operations in the Gulf of Mexico, more aquatic protein is thrown overboard than is contained in the total U.S. catch for human consumption.

Almost half the catches of ocean fish were for several years channeled into the feeding troughs of the developed world, and in the late 1970's around one-third still was going for animal feed. Developed nations secure a lion's share from the oceans. Out of that part of catches which is channeled into human consumption, no less than 65 percent is captured or purchased for consumption by developed nations. Europe, as early as the sixteenth century, stretched out to tap the Newfoundland banks. Following World War II, there was a spectacular oceanic repeat of the global "land grab" by the West. Huge fleets were deployed by the Soviet Union and East and West Europe. The U.S. emerged as the biggest buyer on the world market of fish and fish products, at the rate of two billion dollars per year.

Signs of overfishing abound. Despite declining returns on each catching effort, investments climbed in a frantic attempt to stretch out to new fishing grounds. Japan joined in this grand-scale operation. Fishing was intensified far beyond biological potentials and quotas were implemented greatly above what expert surveys endorsed, totally ignoring the jeopardy to fish stocks. All maneuvering by Japan, Europe, and North America (and to some degree also the Soviet Union) during the 1970's aimed at circumventing any anticipated restrictions. This was done by creating joint companies around the world and engaging in flag changes.

Animal Food Production

The result is that this "last continent" has been tapped, not to feed the developing world, but the reverse. During the 1970's, some efforts were discernible which aimed at channeling more aquatic protein into food and less into animal feed. This reversed a 20 year trend to dispose of a growing percentage of the ocean catches as fish-meal for animal feed. This strong drive had peaked in 1969-70, when half the ocean catches were to feed livestock.

Each Westerner, due to an exorbitant level of animal food production, requires three to five times more grain for daily survival than each person in most of the developing world. Each U.S. citizen requires 1,980 pounds of grain per year. Only 121 pounds enters into bread and other cereal products; 230 pounds goes into the manufacture of beer and other alcoholic drinks. The rest is consumed by livestock. Few developing countries could allow themselves to earmark 40 to 80 percent of their tilled land to animal feedcrops (82 percent in U.K., and 67 percent in the U.S.). Despite the energy and money crises, beef production in developed countries went up by 14 percent, and pork by four percent, between 1973 and 1975.

Population

The population of man's living domain, his biosphere, is not limited to the 1976 figure of 4.2 billion persons. It is actually five times larger and should read 21 billion, out of which livestock, inclusive of poultry, accounts for 16.8 billion. This is measured on the basis of protein intake. The feeding burden of the U.S. is therefore not limited to 215 million, but amounts, in such biological terms, to 1.7 billion. This means that the one billion population increase expected during the 1980's should read five billion, similarly measured.

There are indications that food is not matching these gigantic orders. The backlog in numbers of inadequately fed, now almost two billion, is growing at an alarming pace, with half a billion in the immediate danger zone. Inequities are increasing. The gaps in food consumption are widening at an accelerated rate. Despite expanded acreages, the tilled land available per person in the developing world is declining.

FAO shared for years with the U.S. and the European countries the notion that food production was moving irresistibly upwards, like GNP curves, with a regular annual percentage increment. This was seemingly supported by what happened in the twenty-year period 1952-1972, which gave us a wrong perception. That period was unique in world history. At no time in the last ten centuries was there globally ever a 20-year sequence of such climatically favorable years. This fostered the false belief that technology had removed agriculture from the vagaries of the climate, which throughout history has played havoc with crops and livestock. In 1972-73, the U.S. nonchalantly dipped to the bottom of its grain bins, and only in 1976 was there a substantial refill.

In the aftermath of the Rome Conference, a World Food Council was created. Despite innumerable meetings and the services of highly devoted and competent people, it was only in 1976, three years later, that ten million tons of wheat was pledged to go into contingency storage. Yet, by all gauges, this is a very fragile and inadequate insurance to a world where merely the population growth adds the need of seven million metric tons every year. The annual grain production in the 1970's showed an average fluctuation between years of no less than 25 million metric tons (wheat, seven million). Throughout history every civilization considered the saving from good years to bad ones a prime requisite for survival.

The world will have added to its feeding burden more than one billion persons before 1988, 85 percent of whom will be counted as poor and hungry. This growth in numbers is unprecedented in history. We are adding the equivalent of a new Europe every sixth year, a United States every third year, and a Canada every third month. Asia is adding almost a new Japan every two years. Africa will add close to the equivalent of two United States before the year 2000, and Latin America is the fastest growing area of all. Popular writings and numerous specialist reports either gloss over this issue, or fail to recognize its gravity. China has almost 300 million children, and India around 250 million; we are faced with a young world.

Environmental Issues

The half billion people who live in developing world villages have seemingly been forgotten. HABITAT, the 1976 Vancouver meeting on human settlement sponsored by the U.S., became bogged down in the minutiae of urban planning; villages and rural issues were hardly ever mentioned. This was the greatest flaw of all. The rural and urban world are irrevocably tied to each other, and have to be brought together to restore the woefully disrupted lifelines of survival. Almost every urban dweller remains dependent on food and fuel from rural lands. In the process of focusing on urban affairs, HABITAT overlooked the environmental prerequisites: the biosphere on which the cities depend for their food, air, and water.

Water

Water is unquestionably the most limiting factor in world agriculture. Yet, this century might truly be called that of irrigation; within it, the watered acreage has been more than quadrupled to reach some 230 million hectares. A further doubling is anticipated before the year 2000. The International Hydrological Decade has shown this to be wholly inadequate, and concluded that bringing another 270 million hectares under irrigation, primarily in Asia and Europe, is indispensable, with a price tag of some 2.3 billion dollars. Further tapping of groundwater will be called for, but it must be put in some kind of reasonable line with replenishment in the long run – this has been done very rarely. The exploitation of most groundwater has been proceeding at rates exceeding recharge. The competition with industry for water enters as another decisive force. Many regions cannot afford to return water to the hydrologic cycle via crops when they are forced to restore water for industrial and urban use – a dilemma many arid and semi-arid areas in the U.S. are also facing. Industry and urbanization are more and more on a direct collision course with the food survival basis.

An expansion of irrigation to another 270 million hectares will require massive desalination of ocean water. The involved energy demands are prohibitive, but the salt factor is far more critical. Each acre-foot of such irrigation water results in 42 tons of salt. A ton of wheat creates 35 tons of salt, and a ton of rice three times as much. A growing percentage of so-called irrigation water has to be used for salt removal. Using desalinated water for the irrigation of 100 million hectares (less than half of what is anticipated as needed) would confront mankind with the task of disposing no less than 16 billion tons of salt each year.

Salt is encroaching on tilled lands, and thus causing direct losses in cropland. This is happening in Punjab (both in India and Pakistan), in parts of China, the U.S., and the Middle East. It has forced the creation of costly drainage systems, often coupled with energy-demanding installations for pumping. One-third of all irrigation water in the Nile valley is used for removal of salt, and no longer serves the function of boosting production. Studies conducted during the Hydrological Decade concluded that 45 to 60 percent of all irrigated lands are currently facing declining yields, a phenomenon directly antagonistic to the basic aim of larger crops. A further irony is the fact that increased use of fertilizers elevates the mineral content

of the water and brings the risk levels closer in time. More realistic concern
was expressed at the U.N.'s Mar del Plata (Argentina) Water Conference in
1977 regarding the true role of irrigation.

Erosion

Making deserts bloom is unquestionably one of technology's masterpieces.
Yet, man at the same time created five times larger acreages of deserts, or
some 1.2 billion hectares, whether through negligence, ignorance, or sheer
pressure of numbers in man and livestock. This ignorance of limits is an
outgoing process. No less than 60 to 70 percent of currently-used
pasturelands are threatened through overgrazing, which jeopardizes the plant
cover.

The U.S. must also recognize ecological constraints. The acreage
restrictions through the Soil Bank were a godsend to the semi-arid sections of
the dry prairie, and were in part crucial to avert future repeats of the Dust
Bowl catastrophe of the 1930's. Reports of record crops overlook the fact
that more than 74 million acres (29.5 million hectares) were added to U.S.
tilled land by lifting the Soil Bank restrictions. Such a gain corresponds to
more than the combined tilled lands of France and the United Kingdom (26
million hectares), or 2.3 times that of Italy, or the combined cropland of
both West and East Germany and Poland (27.9 million hectares). Almost no
country in the world could have made such a jump in so brief a time. This has
not only hidden or masked critical adversities in U.S. crop production, but
little is said about the high price paid in soil erosion. In the 1970's, the U.S.
suffered the biggest soil erosion losses since the crisis of the 1930's.

Forests

In man's quest for food and animal feed, more than half the world's forest
cover has vanished, large areas of grasslands have been plowed, and others
turned into deserts through overgrazing. Major groundwater reserves have
been irreversibly consumed, and there is no way of returning these hecatombs
of water which man has transferred to the oceans. In order to accommodate
the future human population, it is anticipated that half of the now remaining
forests will have to yield to the plow or provide badly needed pastures. These
predictions are in poor accord with ambitious plans for expanded forest
production, partly via plantations on tilled land, to fill the needs for both fuel
and forest products. On the whole, the close interdependence of forestry and
agriculture is far too little heeded in development projections.

Land Use

In endless variants, the statement is made that mankind is only using half
of the world's arable land. A doubling is consequently claimed to be within

reach. Such statements have no relationship to the realities of the planet. A ferocious battle is raging between agriculture, forestry, urbanization, industrialization, and road building. Big swaths of land are cut out for transfer of electricity. Recreational areas and wildlife habitats are threatened or are gradually eliminated, in many instances unknowingly. There is also a growing discrepancy between land surveys and actual conditions; the bureaucracies of many countries fail to register lands already being utilized for (or even degraded by) grazing, lumbering, and settlement.

Energy

Energy, land, and labor stand in intricate relationship with each other. The man that tills the fields and tends to livestock utilizes more energy than the industrial worker with all of his energy-devouring machines. By 1972, the energy required to provide the average protein intake of each person in the United Kingdom (31 kilograms/year) had risen to almost one-quarter ton of oil. This corresponds to the total per capita use of fuel energy for all purposes in the developing world. Yet this is only at the farm gate – and not the whole story, when taking into account storage, processing, and marketing. This, in itself, points to the gross global inequities with regard to both food and energy.

The equivalent of 12 or more tons of oil are needed to land an edible ton of shrimp. It is no coincidence that highly nourishing food has become a luxury item – a privilege enjoyed primarily by the U.S., Japan, and France. A ton of eviscerated fish requires an average of one ton of oil for long distance trawling. The truth is that both an agriculture and a fisheries which are beyond the reach of the developing world have been created, and it is highly questionable whether the developed world can persist in upholding this extravagance.

Close to 0.8 tons of petroleum fuel is required annually to feed each person in countries like the U.S. and the United Kingdom. This is three times the average per capita use of fuel for all purposes in the developing world, which cannot emulate such a wasteful food standard. Much energy is used in transporting, storing, processing, packaging, marketing, and cooking food. These sections of the food system in a modern industrial nation require far more energy than the actual growing of crops and raising of livestock. Feeding the urbanized millions hinges on this lifeline, which by necessity has to be made far less energy-costly.

Agriculture is right in the midst of the land tug-of-war between basic food and fuel needs on the one hand, and the demands of industry and transportation within the expanding cities on the other. Spokesmen for so-called "progress" are so totally unaware of the indispensability of tilled land that they look, in all seriousness, towards the day when all surface traffic is placed underground and agriculture has been moved out to ocean platforms. *Terra firma* is to be devoted exclusively to supersonic air traffic and housing. According to this school of thought all food will be made synthetically, presumably also in floating factories to circumvent pollution. This is a telling example of the total absence of even the most basic insight into man's dependence on the biosphere, and, for that matter, the prerequisites for life on spaceship Earth.

Toward the Future

In the overall perspective, the development of the third quarter of the twentieth century was characterized, in part, by impressive achievements in agriculture, fisheries, and technology, but overall strategy has been, and is, lacking. People have been alienating themselves from the stark realities of the world, not recognizing the huge existing disparities.

Misconceptions also pervade the technical response to these urgent needs. There has been far too little regard for biological facts and true economics, as reflected in energy costs. The U.S. practices deep-sea fishing and is developing mariculture. It indulges in devising new protein sources based on costly fabricated foods, such as fish protein concentrates and textured proteins. Yet, the big immediate gains are to be found by reducing waste and spoilage, and expanding the pulse crops. Beans and peas constitute a far cheaper protein supplement to cereals. The raising of legumes has lagged behind, and imbalanced the diet of tens of millions of people. This was their only safeguard against malnutrition engendered by cereal inadequacies and an increasingly lopsided dependence on one kind of crop.

More than one thousand fermented foods are known, of which several constitute good and cheap protein alternatives. Early Oriental civilizations devised methods of enhancing these rich plant protein resources, and making them more accessible to the human gastric system. Nutritionists and planners should take some guidance from these one-time innovations, and greatly improve on them. Vital to both the developed and the developing world will be the need to create supplementary food-producing systems by waste recycling, both in agriculture and forestry, and, more importantly, in the remodeling of the urban ecosystem. The food debate generally has centered around the twin issue of food and people. As long as there was a comfortable margin, more people did mean more food – tilling more land, felling forests, draining and irrigating lands – resorting to increasingly sophisticated methods as agricultural technology evolved. Western man clearly saw the limits emerging in the mid-nineteenth century, and was seriously feeling the pressure. Due to the success of the great migration of people from Europe which followed, the fallacy persisted. More food feeds more people only if an equitable distribution takes place. In far too many cases, only trade has flourished, aggravating food shortages as well as malnutrition. In contrast, it is equally true that adequate food enhances man's productive capability, and also reduces mortality — this in itself results in a reduction of the imperative to have more children.

In analyzing limits and how close we are to them it is, however, urgent to recognize that food and population are intricately interrelated. Four points should be considered: (1) food utilization, (2) resources, (3) nutrition, and (4) diseases. They are all essential considerations in formulating a food strategy, a viable program for the future which can operate within the given limits of our planet. Most food policies have failed to grasp these broader interlinkages. There are no simple solutions; if there were, we would long ago have implemented them. We have to put a stop to restricting bold action, to removing symptoms or applying bandaids; causes must be identified and constructive, long-range measures developed.

How near we are to the limit is measured by the fact that there are, on the entire planet, no more than some 470 million persons who eat as well as an average American. If all globally available food were equally distributed and each one received a U.S. diet, some 960 million would be provided for. This is less than one-fourth of the present world population. If all the tilled land were used for the raising of food instead of animal feed, and diets were accordingly adjusted, almost everyone alive would receive sufficient food. During the 1980's still another billion will have to be provided for, the needs of which will have to be measured against land, water, energy, and fertilizers — all areas within which serious limitations already prevail. A new strategy is therefore urgently called for. The world is actually in a state of emergency.

Our acting and thinking must be based on pertinent facts. They cannot continue to be affected by propagandistic reassurances or exhortations. A broad-based education clarifying the true survival base of each American in terms of land, water, food, and energy requirements must be inculcated. A major goal of education should be to stop this frightening escape from reality by creating a broadly-founded awareness of the basic requirements for human survival.

World Calorie/Protein Needs

Doris H. Calloway

A somewhat heated controversy among nutritionists today relates to the existence of a "protein gap" or a "calorie gap," and there is considerable concern over the establishment of priorities among alternative strategies for dealing with the gap, if one exists. It could be argued that there never was a protein gap, and that, while many people have calorie intakes that are below the amount that would allow them to have an active and fulfilling life, there is probably no calorie gap in the sense of an imbalance between total available calorie supplies and aggregate calorie needs. The nutritional status of human populations can be viewed as an observable characteristic — an output or a consequence — of the total behavior of human ecosystems. If we accept that malnutrition is a systemic failure, then we are concerned also with the intervention that is required to modify the ecosystem and thereby reduce malnutrition.

Protein Requirements

For years, it was believed that there was a protein gap — that is, there was a critical short-fall between the supplies of protein available in the world and the needs of people for protein. This was a result of where standards for protein intake were placed (on the high side of physiologic requirement), and how standards were interpreted. In the 1970's, serious controversy arose as to whether or not lower standards were adequate. The reason for the controversy was that an expert group convened by the U.N.'s Food and Agriculture Organization and World Health Organization (FAO/WHO) lowered the protein allowances to a new, so called "safe level of intake" in a 1973 report (FAO/WHO, 1973). They thereby snapped shut the protein gap. That action launched a number of debates — some in the literature (Scrimshaw, 1976), and many rather heated — about whether or not the new levels were correct, and whether or not there was a protein gap.

In the early days of nutrition studies, standards for protein were really very high. This refers to those elaborated before the 1900's, by Voit and Rubner in Germany, and even earlier, by Smith in England, and Atwater in the U.S. All these experts stated that protein intake ought to be on the order of 100-150 grams a day. They arrived at this conclusion by using one of the possible methods of establishing standards: observed intakes of healthy people. The nature of a sampled population is important; in this case, they

[82]

were laborers. Smith studied cotton workers, and one of his criteria in selecting a sample population was that individuals should be involved in labor that earned them their own support and which was valued by the society. Thus, he eliminated both ends of the economic spectrum, the intellectuals and the rich who sat much of the day, and the under- or unemployed poor. Voit observed a somewhat broader population — soldiers, agricultural workers, and so forth. All these active people ate about 100-150 grams of protein a day, and they appeared to be in good health, so it was concluded that that was what the protein requirement was.

Nitrogen Balance

This high figure was challenged from time to time. One of the early challenges in 1901 came from Sivén, in Scandinavia, who carried out what probably was the first nitrogen balance experiment intended to determine what human requirements actually are. Nitrogen balance is the difference between measured nitrogen (.16 x protein) intake and the output in urine, feces, and from the skin and miscellaneous routes. Negative balance (output>intake) means a loss from the body, and positive balance means protein storage. He reported balance in adults when they ate 25 grams of egg protein a day. In that same period (1905-1910), Chittenden in the U.S. undertook studies of many subjects whom he maintained for long periods of time on low protein diets — he himself followed one and advised everyone to do so. Chittenden stated that the true minimum requirement was 39 grams of protein a day for an adult, but, recognizing that there are differences between people and differences in the kinds of protein eaten, he suggested an allowance of 50 grams a day. These lower figures were then challenged, and a controversy was launched in very much the same vein as in the 1970's.

Studies by McCay

The controversy was beneficial because it made opposing forces seek other indicators of proper protein nutrition than simply nitrogen balance. A dominant critic was an Englishman named McCay. He was among the first to link nutrition with height and weight, morbidity, and life expectancy. He looked at groups of students in Bengal; some were Eurasians and some Bengali, and they ate different diets — the Eurasians a more typically Western diet and the Bengalis a rice-based diet. The Bengalis were smaller and had poorer health indices; their protein intakes were nearly the same as Chittenden's recommendation on a body weight basis. (Average body weight was lower in the early 1900's than the 1970's and Chittenden's recommendation was equivalent to 0.94 grams per kilogram of body weight.) The Bengali students eating a rice diet had a very low protein intake but were quite small, so their intake was 1.25 grams per kilogram. Chittenden answered

McCay's criticism by stating that much of the poor rating of the Bengalis probably related to the fact that their diet was monotonous, and that it was not very well balanced. That was a remarkable statement for 1910 because vitamins had not yet been discovered, but Chittenden recognized that a balance of foods was required to maintain health. Controversy in the 1970's has involved the same issues. Is nitrogen balance an adequate criterion? How do other dietary proteins compare with egg protein? What better criteria of adequacy can be identified?

It is difficult to know what people should have in their diets. It is also worth noting that, in spite of the 70-year debate among scientists, there is no evidence that people have eaten any differently because of expert views and recommendations. People appear simply to select what they like from among the foods they can produce, or from those available in the market at prices they can afford. Physiologically, what governs the amount of food eaten is the energy need, but what governs the type of food eaten is preference.

Protein Allowances

Protein allowance figures have also been established by various committees. The first internationally recognized standards were from the League of Nations in 1936, and were based on ordinary diets. The first set of recommendations by the U.S. National Academy of Sciences/National Research Council (NAS/NRC) were formulated at the end of World War II, and they were similar to the League of Nations recommendations.

An FAO/WHO committee met in 1955 and drew up a set of recommendations which they gave in terms of a hypothetical reference protein, a protein of good quality: egg. A 1965 committee used as reference a hypothetical protein of 100 percent utilization quality. The previously-mentioned FAO/WHO 1973 report stipulated "safe levels of intake" in the form of egg or milk proteins. In all three of these reports, directions were provided for adjustment of dietary allowances of protein according to the mix of food proteins in the ordinary diet.

Recommended allowances of protein, both American and international, have been lowered since the 1930's. The reduction in allowances for young children occurred in the 1965 revision of international standards, and the 1973 allowances for children are not significantly different from the 1965 figures. The 1973 committee did, however, recommend much lower allowances for teenagers and adults. Allowances for teenagers are less than half the original recommendation by the League of Nations, and the adult values are lower still. The value established for adult males is 0.57 grams of egg or milk protein per kilogram of body weight, or for dietary protein with a score of 70 (relative to egg/milk), 0.8 grams per kilogram. For women it is slightly lower, about 0.75 grams per kilogram. In 1973, the National Research

Council recommended allowances of 0.8 grams per kilogram body weight for both men and women, a figure far below the average American intake of protein.

National Protein Needs

National protein needs have been computed from these allowance figures, taking into account the demographic characteristics of the population and adult body weights. The figure so computed may be expressed as total national need or as per capita requirements for the country. Common practice is to compare these calculated requirements with food production or disappearance statistics to determine if national "intake" meets recommended allowances. All such calculations can show is whether or not sufficient food protein is available for a country as a whole; without knowledge of food distribution, it is not possible to derive valid estimates of the risk of protein deficiency in the population. However, national protein availability figures based on the higher recommended allowances indicated that some countries did not have protein supplies adequate to meet needs. This gap disappeared when needs were recalculated according to the 1973 allowances.

In terms of national statistics, only changes in the allowances for older children and adults have any significant impact on calculated per capita needs because of their proportional contribution to the population, coupled with larger body size. It matters but little where the allowances for very young children are placed, because of their small size, and the allowances for pregnancy and lactation have little impact because of the relatively small numbers involved.

There are other problems in attempting to estimate the magnitude of protein deficiency, using allowance figures as a base, which are not fully appreciated. These stem from the manner in which recommended allowances are derived. Expert committees attempt to derive a figure that represents the average requirements of a population according to some stated criterion, and then add two standard deviations to that figure, so that if an individual intake meets that level there is a very low probability that needs are not met. This procedure is acceptable for most nutrients, most vitamins and minerals, and protein, because there is thought to be little risk from excess intake compared to needs. Experts have taken a different view of calorie allowances because intakes over or under true needs have serious problems associated with them. Comparing an individual's intake with a recommended allowance can, at best, provide an estimate of the risk of deficiency, and the risk assignment is different for calorie than for protein comparisons. The literature is filled with studies that conclude that people are at nutritional risk because intake falls below two-thirds the recommended daily allowance, yet that level is above the *average* requirement, so 50 percent of the population would have needs fully met. Thus, these comparisons tend to lead to erroneously high estimates of deficiency risk.

Calorie Requirements

Simple calculation of nutrient density requirements (nutrient:calorie ratios) gives spuriously high figures for the average person because of the different bases of the allowances for calories and other nutrients. On the other hand, given that food is available, people tend to meet or exceed their needs for calories. There is no known physiological drive for any nutrient except salt, and thus no guarantee that a person with high protein requirements is necessarily the highest consumer of protein. As the factors that affect calorie and protein requirements are not the same in totality, there is also no guarantee that the person with a high calorie requirement also has a high protein requirement; the converse could well be true. Thus, the percentage of calories derived from protein in the individual's diet is not a safe predictor of adequacy unless the obverse extreme situations are used as a basis of calculation (lowest calories, highest protein). In calculating population food supplies, probable distribution of calorie and protein-yielding foods among consumers also must be taken into account, and these calculations lead to unrealistically high and virtually unattainable percentages of protein and calories in national diets (Beaton and Swiss, 1974; Payne, 1975).

None of the national calculations taken alone can yield reliable estimates of protein or calorie deficiency, because we do not know who eats what. There are undoubtedly people in all populations whose habitual intake does not meet calorie or protein allowances. There are others whose intake does not meet their individual physiologic requirement. This seems a contradiction in terms because if, for example, true calorie needs are not being met, then the person should waste away and die. Many do. But others survive by being undersized and less physically active than they should be for full functional competency in society. What is implied by saying that children's calorie intakes are below requirement is that they cannot grow to their genetic potential, they cannot run and play, and they cannot explore their environment and develop fully. The cost of habitually low intakes by adults is to be counted in their legacy of childhood undernutrition, coupled with their present lessened ability to produce or procure their own subsistence, to care for their families, and to contribute to the life of their communities. In the case of calories, more importantly perhaps than for any specific nutrient, we must begin to define "requirement" not simply according to biological criteria, but rather according to a range of socially significant functions.

Food Supply and Malnutrition

However the figures are derived, it is clear that some countries have a higher per capita supply of calories and protein than do others. Population surveys reveal that far too many households in far too many countries have real gaps between their food supplies and those intakes thought to be compatible with growth, health, and a fulfilling life. Studies of individuals reveal that many do suffer from the effects of acute and chronic shortages of food, and especially of foods of good nutritional quality. Food shortage is only one deprivation experience of most of those affected; they lack also the range of goods and services that societies can and should provide.

As long as authorities are allowed to view the pervasive problem of deprivation in terms of "food availability," it is unlikely that correct action will be taken. Programs designed to improve food production will result in sustained improvement of the nutritional state of those malnourished only if production is increased by strategies that increase the productivity of those who cannot now provide for themselves. Giving food, such as dispensing milk to children in Chile, commodity foods to impoverished Americans, and cereal grains to poor nations, and other philanthropy, only buys a little time.

References

Beaton, G. H., and L. D. Swiss
1974   Evaluation of the nutritional quality of food supplies: prediction of "desirable" or "safe" protein-calorie ratios. *American Journal of Clinical Nutrition 27*:485.

FAO/WHO
1973   *Energy and Protein Requirements*. Report of a Joint FAO/WHO Ad Hoc Expert Committee, FAO Nutrition Meetings Report Series No. 52, Rome, Italy.

Payne, P. R.
1975   Safe protein-calorie ratios in diets. The relative importance of protein and energy intake as causal factors in malnutrition. *American Journal of Clinical Nutrition 28*:281.

Scrimshaw, N.
1976   Shattuck Lecture—Strengths and Weaknesses of the Committee Approach. An analysis of past and present recommended dietary allowances for protein in health and disease. *New England Journal of Medicine 294*:136.

World Food Requirements
And The Search For
New Protein Resources

Max Milner, Nevin S. Scrimshaw, and D.I.C. Wang

Background

Developments on the world food scene in the 1970's sharply intensified interest in research aimed at increasing food supply. As a consequence of these events, questions have been raised in the U.S. about its own longer-term capability in food and protein production to fill domestic needs, to sustain major export demands, and to respond to urgent international emergency feeding programs.

In this context, the National Science Foundation (NSF) found itself receiving, primarily from universities, requests to finance projects for research into an array of unconventional and novel protein sources. It quickly became evident that there was a lack of information which would permit critical judgment of the relative priorities for such funding requests. It was clear, furthermore, that, in the foreseeable future, the bulk of U.S. and world food supplies would have to come from traditional agricultural sources. Logically, therefore, fundamental and applied research for improving the productivity of conventional agriculture would have to have the greatest emphasis, and priorities assigned to unconventional proteins would need to be judged in this context.

With these considerations in mind, NSF proposed to the Department of Nutrition and Food Science at the Massachusetts Institute of Technology (MIT) a study to analyze, in some detail, the status and potential of all relevant protein resources, and to provide recommendations for carefully selected projects and priorities worthy of research support. The MIT summary report and recommendations to NSF on protein resources research appeared early in 1976. It may be worth noting that almost precisely at the time this MIT study was initiated, the National Academy of Sciences (NAS) received from President Ford, as a consequence of Secretary of State Kissinger's commitments to the U.N. World Food Conference, a request to develop specific recommendations for how the nation's agricultural research and developmental capabilities could be applied to world food supply problems. The Academy's summary report appeared in the summer of 1977.

The MIT study recognized that many aspects of protein resources research are already receiving attention, principally from the U.S. Department of

[88]

Agriculture, from the state universities and land grant colleges with their associated experiment stations, and from industry. Nevertheless, study team members were convinced that important areas of research vital to strengthening U.S. food and protein productivity are either inadequately funded, or are entirely neglected, in terms of available research support. Also, in the decades ahead, notwithstanding the recent improvement of food availability in international markets, there is likely to be a need to supplement conventional agriculture, and some resources should be directed toward research on possible unconventional protein sources, as well as toward innovative areas of agricultural research not now receiving adequate attention and support. These are the primary areas which the MIT study delineated, and recommended for NSF research emphasis.

Organization of the Study

In addition to a Policy Advisory Committee, various groups of specialists, organized into committees or working groups, developed the information needed to evaluate problems affecting protein production and the status of various resources and their research needs. Establishment of research priorities required an estimation of both domestic and export protein demand for the remainder of the century, and an assessment of the likelihood that these demands would be satisfactorily met from traditional U.S. crop, livestock, and fisheries resources. Problems which were analyzed generally included nutritional quality and its assessment, toxicology and food safety, processing technology, energy constraints, plant genetic potentials, nitrogen fixation, marketing of protein foods, and legal, regulatory, and political constraints which may influence introduction of novel proteins. Protein resource areas for which status analyses and research recommendations were prepared included grain crops, cereal proteins, oilseeds, food legumes, livestock production, dairy products, meat, poultry and eggs, aquatic proteins, potatoes, nonphotosynthetic single-cell protein (SCP), photosynthetic SCP, leaf proteins, and chemical synthesis of nutrients.

Significant Determinants of Research Recommendations

Review by the Policy Advisory Committee of the extensive documentation prepared for this study suggested that there were a number of significant conclusions or hypotheses which had considerable relevance when identifying research recommendations and priorities. The following are pertinent:

1. U.S. agriculture will continue in the foreseeable future to supply in abundance the protein foods and feeds to which this country has become accustomed, but it will obviously do so with rising costs and increasing pressure on our land, energy, and environmental resources.

2. Appropriate research and technological development must be pursued

more vigorously to achieve increases in productivity, protein quality, and
protein quantity of primary food crops and aquatic resources, to meet both
domestic demand and export opportunities.

3. A strengthening of food and agricultural research capabilities will be
necessary to ensure continued growth of food export, which is a major
contributor to the maintenance of favorable U.S. trade balances. With
adequate research support, and if other appropriate policies are adopted, U.S.
food export capacity should increase at a rate following the trend established
prior to 1972 until at least 1985.

4. The food and feed demands of affluent industrial countries will
continue to increase and will exert growing pressure on food resources
available in international markets.

5. Even with probable improvements, the agricultural production
capacities of some major developing countries will not soon be adequate to
feed their growing populations. They will need to import food for many years
to come and surplus producers such as the U.S. and Canada will play a leading
role in supplying these needs, largely on regular commercial terms.

6. When developing countries improve their own agriculture and food
production capabilities, not only will the nutritional status of their
populations be increased, but, experience has shown, they will also tend to
increase their commercial food purchases in international markets.

7. In the foreseeable future, the relative cost of proteins (e.g., meat,
soybeans) for human and animal feeding is likely to increase more rapidly
than the cost for staple sources of food or feed energy (e.g., corn, wheat).

8. The foreseeable domestic and world demand for soybeans as a primary
protein resource, notwithstanding increasing production in other countries
such as Brazil, will grow faster than for other food or feed crops. While a
major breakthrough in soybean yields may occur, it is not likely to be
effective in the next ten years. This will stimulate interest in alternative
protein sources of both conventional and unconventional types.

9. It is likely that new and more productive grain crops will be
developed, particularly from intergeneric crossing of cereals, of which triticale
is a prototype.

10. The marketplace must reflect the increased value of crops offering
improved protein quality and quantity if farmers are to be persuaded to
produce them. Incentives may also be needed to encourage commercial
initiatives by the seed industry and others directed toward more rapid
development of improved food crop varieties.

11. The increasing costs of agricultural food production may eventually
encourage the use of unconventional techniques for protein production which
are not now commercially competitive.

12. The reclaiming of organic wastes of all kinds for food and feed use is a major priority.

13. The development and application of innovative food processing techniques, and of new science and technology, to the production of protein foods, will require fair and objective regulatory standards and procedures on the part of federal regulatory agencies such as the Food and Drug Administration, the U.S. Department of Agriculture, and the Environmental Protection Agency.

14. Acceptance by the consumer of novel protein foods to any significant extent will require innovative marketing and promotional approaches which, to be effective, must go beyond emphasis on nutritional benefits.

15. Adoption and enforcement by many countries of the 200-mile offshore fishing limit will remove some prime fishing areas from free international exploitation, and thus may affect protein supplies and prices in international markets. Over 30 countries, including the U.S., have already adopted this limit.

Common Problems and Issues Requiring Research

Nutrition

Adequate assessment of the protein problem is handicapped by lack of knowledge in two fundamental areas: (1) human requirements for protein at different ages and in different physiological states, and (2) the evaluation of protein quality of foods. These issues are further complicated by increasing evidence that both are greatly affected by calorie excess as well as calorie deficit.

It is apparent that the recommendations for protein requirements by the U.N.'s Food and Agriculture Organization and World Health Organization (FAO/WHO) and, similarly, those of the National Academy of Sciences/National Research Council's Food and Nutrition Board, do not provide an adequate basis for determination of a safe, practical allowance for either individuals or populations, especially under adverse environmental circumstances.

There is an urgent need to develop and apply improved methods of protein quality evaluation which are sufficiently rapid and inexpensive to be used by the food industry, by regulatory agencies, and by plant breeders seeking to develop new crop varieties of high nutritional value. These methods should be feasible for use with the extremely small samples likely to be available. For novel protein sources in general, and particularly for both novel and conventional sources subject to extensive processing, evaluation of protein quality is especially important.

Toxicology

Toxic factors, which even in small amounts may pose a threat to animals and humans, occur in many widely-used foods unless the foods are specially processed or restricted in use. A group of inhibitors of protein digesting enzymes — e.g., the hemagglutinins (lectins) and trypsin inhibitors, which are themselves protein in nature — occur widely in food legumes (peas, beans) and oilseeds (soybeans). Fortunately, most of these inhibitors are deactivated by heat during processing. Cyanogens (glucosides containing hydrocyanic acid) occur in significant quantities in foods as diverse as lima beans, almonds, cassava, and sorghum. Saponins are toxins occurring in over 400 species of the plant kingdom — including sugar beets, spinach, and asparagus. Gossypol is a toxic pigment found in cottonseed (*Gossypium*). Favism is a genetically-linked disease caused by ingestion of a toxin in broad beans (*Vicia faba*). Lathyrism can be severely debilitating and even fatal in humans ingesting the legumes of the *Lathyrus* (sweet pea) species. Goitrogens, usually in the form of thioglucosides, are present in the *Brassica* species (cabbage, turnips, and mustard). A variety of antivitamins also occur in plant foods.

In addition to natural food toxins, substances which are potentially hazardous to man and animals may be added to foods as preservatives or coloring and flavoring agents. Some toxicants may be introduced unintentionally through the use of pesticides or fungicides. Food-safety problems associated with incomplete removal of mycotoxins and other microbial toxins are well recognized.

In many cases, studies on experimental animals alone are not sufficient to detect all possibilities of adverse reactions in man, since symptoms which may appear in human trials may not arise in experimental animal tests.

The need for toxicity studies is particularly evident with such proposed new protein sources as single-cell protein from both photosynthetic and nonphotosynthetic organisms, forage and leaf protein concentrates, and new legume and oilseed sources.

Innovative Technology for Protein Utilization

Traditional techniques for isolating proteins for processing into food are based mainly on extraction of a primary product (such as oil from oilseeds) with little concern for the integrity of the protein. As a result, the by-product proteins may become unsuitable for many useful applications. New technology should be developed to more effectively retain the desired properties of the protein.

The basic properties of proteins from various sources require study in order to relate their molecular properties to their physical properties, and their physical properties to their functional (or performance) properties, through theoretical or correlative techniques. The critical molecular properties needing identification include molecular weights and distribution; ionization properties; reactive side chains; and primary, secondary, tertiary, and quaternary structure and morphology. Physical aspects to be characterized include hydration properties such as solubility in various media; suspendability; swelling; gelling; and rheological properties such as viscosity or apparent viscosity; yield stress; time dependency; shear dependency; and creep and relaxation. Thermal aspects include gelation and coagulation, while surface properties include hydrophilic and lipophilic properties, and surface absorption and adsorption.

For data on performance characteristics, studies are required on reactivity between starch, fat, flavoring, and other food ingredients, and on relationships between performance properties and chemical and physical properties.

Examples of process research would be concentration and isolation of protein materials, and methodologies for restructuring protein materials, or combining proteins with other materials. The effect of processing conditions on physical properties, and the influence of changes in the latter on organoleptic (taste, smell) characteristics of the final product, both need to be studied.

Potentials for Improving Protein Quality in Plants by Genetic Means

Geneticists and plant breeders have, in recent years, succeeded in developing or identifying mutations in corn, barley, and sorghum, which have significantly higher relative levels of lysine, as well as favorable alterations in levels of other amino acids, in their seed proteins. This achievement raises questions of the extent to which similar mutations are possible in other grains or crop plants, and also brings up the question of the ultimate limits of this kind of genetic manipulation.

The single gene mutations which substantially increase lysine content in corn, barley, and sorghum involve changes in the proportions of the few protein species that normally constitute the storage protein complement of seeds, but apparently without affecting their amino acid composition. Apparently the situation is different in the case of rice and wheat. Rice has a low proportion of prolamine to begin with, and no prolamine-depressing mutation would have much effect in altering amino acid composition. Wheat does contain a sizable proportion of its total seed protein as prolamine, but mutants which cause its repression are recessive. The hexaploid nature of the wheat species combines genomes of three closely related diploid species. The probability that a similar mutation would occur in all the others at the same time is obviously extremely small.

The suppression of the synthesis of less desirable protein fractions, and the secondary increase in synthesis of fractions with greater biological value, may also be effective in legumes which, in the case of *Phaseolus,* show similar storage protein heterogeneity.

Biological Nitrogen Fixation

Enhancement of biological nitrogen fixation, whether symbiotic or nonsymbiotic, requires greater understanding of the processes themselves, and of the organisms which bring about the processes. The protein nature of the nitrogenase complex that catalyzes nitrogen fixation in organisms is fairly well understood. Research is needed to determine the crystalline enzyme components, the role of ATP in the system, the mechanism whereby iron and molybdenum are incorporated into the enzyme, and the energetics and kinetics of the overall reaction.

The genes coding for nitrogenase in bacteria have been successfully transferred from one species to another. Thus, the genetic potential exists for extending nitrogen-fixing capability to a variety of economically important organisms.

In nitrogen-fixing legumes, a better understanding is needed of the genetics of both the host species and the bacterial endophytes. In the breeding of improved legumes, insufficient attention has been given to host/endophyte relationships. Useful application of biological nitrogen fixation to grasses requires better understanding of the genetic and biochemical compatibility of host and endophytes.

Limitations to increased yield in legumes seem to be related not only to conditions affecting the availability of useful *Rhizobium* strains and the adequacy of present innoculation techniques, but, in the case of soybeans at least, to an insufficiency in photosynthate energy required to maintain optimum nitrogen inputs. A broad spectrum of research is needed on the many physiological and agronomic aspects of nitrogen-fixing systems of known or potential significance.

Specific Protein Resources

Grain Crops for Food and Feed

The tremendous and relatively unexplored genetic diversity of cereal grains provides great promise for expanded food and protein production. An accelerated genetic search for increased protein quantity and quality in the major cereals requires medium- and long-term funding. These genetic questions also call for considerable research in fundamental scientific areas relating to genetics, and in this respect represent an appropriate area of NSF concern. For example, comprehensive biochemical research on the uptake and translocation of nitrogen in crop plants, as well as related seed protein metabolism (especially in the cereal grains) can lead to the development of genetic or other means for increasing seed protein quantity and quality. There is a need for expanded basic studies on the biochemical aspects of plant physiology and metabolism.

Rapid, accurate procedures for screening a variety of crops for protein nutritional quality need to be developed, for use by plant breeders, to select superior lines. Such research requires reevaluation or review of bioassay procedures and their pertinence to human and livestock animal requirements.

Increasing soybean yields by breeding requires use of germ plasm from mainland Asia. Another approach to the soybean yield problem is to determine the cause or mechanism of oxidative photorespiration in vegetative soybeans and other legumes. This mechanism limits carbon fixation and, therefore, grain yield.

Symbiotic association of nitrogen-fixing bacteria with roots of certain grasses and corn suggest that similar associations with cereals can be identified or developed, so as to allow large savings in energy because of reduced need for nitrogen fertilizer.

Cereal Protein Technology

The normal abundance in the U.S. of low-cost grains and their underutilized by-products suggests the desirability of initiating greater scientific and technological efforts to upgrade their food use and nutritional value.

New technologies and processes need to be perfected for separating upgraded protein products from grains and their industrial by-products. These methods would include improved techniques for producing stable and edible protein concentrates from wheat milling by-products, better methods for separation of wheat gluten by aqueous processes, and separation of edible protein isolates from other cereals and their by-products. Along with an improved technology for preparing protein concentrates, new food processing applications for proteins in formulated food products should also be developed.

Research is under way in these areas, but with low priority status, in the U.S. Department of Agriculture, the state institutions, and some food industry laboratories. To stimulate this important application of technology, an economic and marketing feasibility survey is needed.

Oilseed Proteins

Soybeans represent the single largest source of oilseed protein for both animal and human consumption, and most technology for the food use of oilseed proteins relates to soybeans and a spectrum of products derived from them. A number of other oilseeds, e.g. cottonseed, peanuts, sunflowers, rapeseed, and sesame, have potential for similar utilization; however, the necessary technology for production of food-grade products from these materials is not fully developed. Additional research is needed on all these oilseeds, including soybeans, to solve problems involving flavor, functionality, color, antinutritional factors, processing technology, and many other factors.

Research and development in six food processing and utilization areas will be essential if oilseed proteins are to achieve maximum acceptance in human foods. Specifically:

1. protein and nonprotein component interactions during processing must be identified;
2. fundamental physical and chemical characteristics of the proteins of oilseeds, as related to their functional properties, need to be studied;
3. screening methods must be developed for determining functional properties of oilseed proteins with respect to their utilization in food systems;
4. identification of components responsible for undesirable flavors and development of processing technology to eliminate these from food products is essential;
5. investigation should be undertaken into modifying the functionality of oilseed proteins by physical, chemical, or enzymatic means; and
6. assessment is needed of the level at which the presence of flatus-producing oligosaccharides in oilseed products assumes practical significance, and technology to minimize this problem needs to be developed.

Food Legumes

Taking into account the major problems that need to be overcome in production, utilization, and marketing of food legumes, the following recommendations are offered:

In food legume *production,* research is needed to:

1. overcome genetic-physiological barriers to higher seed and protein yield;
2. improve control of and resistance to disease and insect pests;
3. promote greater efficiency in cultural systems; and
4. reduce the deleterious effects of adverse environmental factors.

In *utilization* research, the most urgent priorities are to:

1. develop convenient and rapid quantitative methods to be used by breeders for the estimation, identification, and removal of undesirable or toxic constituents in legume seeds;
2. develop more rapid and valid methods of estimating the nutritive value of legume proteins, and apply this new technology to the improvement of protein quality in commercial seed types;
3. study combinations of legumes with cereal products and other staple foods, with the objective of improving the nutritional properties and

digestibility of both; and
4. develop improved, stable, processed dry legume products that may be prepared for eating quickly, i.e., with a minimum of energy (fuel) input.

Livestock Production

U.S. animal industries are capable of producing most of the fresh meat consumed in the U.S., plus some for export, until the year 2000. However, in order to do so, great advances will be necessary in the productivity and efficiency of animal production enterprises. These advances can be achieved through increased research in (1) recycling of animal wastes; (2) further use of by-products, wastes, and other alternative feed sources; (3) improvement of animal reproduction and growth efficiency; (4) greater use of forages in animal rations; (5) increased efficiency of nonprotein nitrogen utilization by animals; and (6) development, through breeding programs, of animals which can effectively utilize more forage rations.

Animal Protein from Dairy Products

The supply and utilization of milk in the U.S. dropped from 56,700 million kilograms in the early 1960's (296 kilograms per capita in 1960) to about 53,500 million kilograms in the early 1970's (253 kilograms per capita in 1973). It was estimated at that time that by 1980, per capita dairy food consumption in the U.S. would be down to 237 kilograms.

It is not likely, that is, that U.S. per capita milk consumption will increase. The American consumer perceives no nutritional need for increased dairy consumption, although this conception overlooks the importance of milk as a calcium source. It would take increased government-financed subsidies to produce more, but it is unlikely that the government will take steps to increase production capacity as long as other countries can produce surplus milk more cheaply than the U.S. can. Demands, therefore, will probably be met increasingly by imports.

This situation requires that government-sponsored research on dairy products be strengthened during the 1980's by 30 percent, and industry research by 50 percent. For primary dairy products and for dairy analogs, research and related efforts are needed to:
1. improve quality and convenience of the established products, on the basis of market research guidance;
2. develop new dairy products and concepts which are marketable and competitive with fruit juices and soft drinks;
3. perfect a rapid, automated cheese production and ripening process which would increase the competitiveness of cheese in both domestic and export markets;

4. develop new processing and preservation methods for milk, so as to increase its useful storage life, reduce bulk, and make milk a significant protein resource suitable for worldwide shipment and trade;

5. develop dairy analogs based on vegetable proteins;

6. conduct nutritional studies to clarify the role of nonlipid dietary components, as well as milkfat and dietary cholesterol, with respect to coronary heart disease;

7. optimize the food technological utility and functionality of dairy proteins as replacement proteins in fabricated foods, taking into account safety as well as nutritional factors; and

8. undertake economic and marketing studies to determine both the feasibility of increasing U.S. dairy exports, and the most favorable product mix of natural and analog dairy products.

Areas suggested for research into secondary dairy products include (1) chemical modification and upgrading of whey proteins into useful new products; (2) whey protein fractionation and characterization; (3) fundamental investigation into improving sensory and organoleptic properties of whey for applications in foods; (4) clarification of galactose metabolism in humans as a first step to wider utilization of lactose; and (5) development of whey products for the world market as protein supplements to upgrade protein-deficient diets.

All the agencies concerned with dairy research − i.e., industry, the federal government, and the state universities and experiment stations − have roles and responsibilities in attacking these problems more vigorously. The call for innovations in food science also suggests that NSF could usefully support selected projects in the areas indicated.

Animal Protein from Meat, Poultry and Eggs

There is great potential for expanded development, production, and utilization in the meat and egg industries. The utilization of this potential will depend on research and development inputs, and on the realism of regulatory constraints in terms of risk-cost-benefit considerations. It is also apparent that energy availability and cost, environmental issues, and governmental policy decisions will have far-reaching effects on the future availability of meat and eggs.

A significant expansion of the supply of animal protein for human consumption could be brought about as a result of research into use of animal tissues which are at present diverted from the market by health or palatability considerations, or by government restrictions on otherwise safe and nutritious products.

Many packing-house raw materials, such as visceral organs, are currently processed into livestock and pet feeds. Processes similar to those used to produce fish protein concentrates have been developed for the production of edible meat protein concentrates from the various offal tissues. However, further studies are needed in this area, as well as review of regulations to permit their use as human food.

Technical knowledge now available to the meat industry could result in increasing the output of processed meat products by over 50 percent, through appropriate extension or supplementation with plant proteins.

Consumers are concerned with the possible relationship of diet to coronary heart disease. Attention centers on cholesterol and animal fats. Because the consumption of nutritious foods may be inhibited by adverse publicity based on inadequate scientific evidence, it is imperative that well-planned, long-range studies be implemented to clarify these questions.

Rigid and frequently outdated standards of identity discourage the development of new or improved products, which could extend the quality and variety of the national protein supply. Other standards – e.g. microbiological standards – increase cost to the consumer without demonstrating improvements in product quality or safety as a result of their enforcement. Overregulation, in short, adds to product cost, channeling much industry research funding into matters concerned primarily with regulatory compliance.

Broad areas of research have been receiving attention by industry, the federal government, and the state universities and experiment stations, but such activity requires far greater support from funding sources than has been the case heretofore. As regards relatively basic research, there are a number of areas where NSF support would help stimulate the solution of serious and longstanding problems.

Aquatic Proteins

Most of the U.S. fishery stocks traditionally used by Americans for food are either fully exploited or depleted. There are, however, species even within the present, limited economic control zone – not to mention the larger resources within the proposed 200-mile zone – which have remained largely un- or underexploited. It is estimated, for example, that between 100,000 and 500,000 metric tons of capelin could be landed yearly on the northwestern Atlantic coast. This fish could be offered in the form of engineered or fabricated foods which would be more familiar to the public. Squid, likewise, is most suitably utilized in textured and engineered food products.

Much more needs to be known about the biology and behavior patterns of aquatic animals, and techniques need to be developed for locating, harvesting, preserving, and processing this resource. Polyculture, which relies on the growing-together of a number of fish species of varying feeding types, presents opportunities for attaining very high yields per hectare by taking advantage of symbiotic relationships among the different species. The high yields in such systems can be maintained without competing with nonruminant farm animals for feed. Species with maximum productivity potential in warm freshwater pond polyculture systems include carp, buffalofish, tilapia, white amur, mullet, milkfish, and catfish.

Capture fisheries represent the major focus of aquatic protein resource development. Antarctic krill, for example, is the single largest natural source of animal protein in the world, and probably 45 million metric tons of it could be harvested yearly without compromising the availability of the resource. In view of the lead taken by the Soviet Union, and, to a lesser extent, by Japan, in krill harvesting and utilization, the U.S. must now decide what commitments it should undertake in the management and utilization of this resource. It seems prudent to advise allocation of funds at levels sufficient at least to undertake a technical and economic feasibility study of U.S. participation in and utilization of the krill harvest.

Financial and political decisions to support research and development will have to be made by the government, since industry will not initially invest the hundreds of millions of dollars required to perfect the tools needed to produce and utilize increased tonnage of raw aquatic material. New types of suitably equipped fishing vessels will have to be designed and constructed. New methods of locating, harvesting, preserving, and processing must be developed. New toxicological and nutritional information will be necessary to develop regulations for monitoring the quality and safety of the new aquatic food products. Investigations will be needed in biology, genetics, animal nutrition, and ecology of aquatic organisms. NSF could most appropriately provide funding for studies in oceanography, ecology, physiology, basic biology, and other background areas.

Potatoes

The potato has protein levels comparable to those of cereal grains; indeed, cultivars containing 17-18 percent protein (dry weight basis) have been identified. The crop, clearly, does not merit the status of a "poor man's" energy food.

With the introduction of new potato varieties, this crop's yields per hectare have increased nearly 300 percent in the past 20 years. Through intensified breeding studies, exploration of hybridization should be continued, in order to expand adaptation, and improve disease and insect resistance, nutritive value, and yield; the ideal polyploid level for optimum productivity should be determined.

Systematic study is needed on factors affecting productivity and nutritional quality. These factors include optimum stage of maturity, effects of fertilization and irrigation, and possible benefits of multiple cropping with early and late maturing varieties, and with other crops. (This last factor is relevant especially to potato culture in warmer environments.)

Researchers need to analyze potatoes for quantity and quality of various proteins, evaluate their amino acid composition, and determine whether or not breeding can alter protein ratios, so as to improve the overall protein nutritive quality. Simple screening methods for protein quality and quantity are needed to assist breeders in analyzing large potato populations.

Much work also needs to be done on the reclaiming and upgrading of potato processing wastes, with emphasis on recovery of proteins and amino acids.

Nonphotosynthetic Single-Cell Protein

The role of single-cell protein (SCP) as a supplement to the world protein supply is now well established. Research and development on SCP production have been intense since the 1960's, and as a consequence a number of large SCP plants are in operation for animal feed production; several more are under construction. The problems being addressed today relate to second and third generation processes for SCP production for both animal feed and human food.

No single raw material or organism will provide the ultimate SCP process. Consequently, it is essential to evaluate, in parallel, several process alternatives, to appreciate fully the flexibility available in the use of SCP. There is no specific recommendation of substrates, but it is clearly the overall view of the experts that alcohols and cellulose hold the greatest potential for the U.S., and therefore should receive priority consideration.

It is believed that cell yield is the single most important economic factor in the fermentation process, and that great stress should be placed, in practice, on approaching the theoretical fermentation yield. Improved processes for RNA removal would involve study of RNA levels in cells, the role and activation of endogenous ribonucleases, and their control by means of genetic and cell physiology factors.

More efficient use could be made of the proteins within the cell if economical means for their recovery were available. Selective isolation of proteins would also be a method of avoiding the RNA problem. Studies are needed of SCP engineering properties, interactions with food constituents, and use in structure-forming operations. Dewatering and drying comprise one of the most significant cost factors in the overall process. Study is needed on membrane processes, improved methods of mass transfer, and the effect of drying on functional properties.

Research on nonphotosynthetic SCP clearly needs much wider support in the U.S., in order to increase production of protein and other useful products, especially from waste. Such research and development activities in the U.S. are confined to industry and a few universities. The growing urgency in the U.S. for waste recovery and recycling – the need to reprocess livestock animal waste and manure for refeeding is only one example – suggests a priority area for NSF funding.

Photosynthetic Single-Cell Protein

Photosynthetic SCP is produced in the cells of microscopic plants (algae) which grow in suspension in the waters of shallow, illuminated ponds. These ponds contain culture medium which consists of simple salts – such as carbonates, nitrates, and phosphates – dissolved in water. Depending on the genus, the cells may be separated from the growth medium by screening, filtration, coagulation either by flotation or sedimentation, and centrifugation.

During the 1980's steps should be taken to:

1. study the relationship of algal species to algal nutritional characteristics, including protein quality, and the influence of ratios of critical substrate nutrients, including consideration of water quality factors;
2. study productivity as a function of species, predators and pathogens, nutrient mix, physical parameters such as detention period, mixing, recirculation, and waste as a source of nutrients; and
3. study processing of algae to produce various products, including decolorized and bleached algae, algal pigments, and spun algal protein; and study algal preservation by dehydration, canning, drying, freezing, and freeze drying.

Leaf Protein

Green leaves are the largest producers of protein in the world, supplying protein to other plant tissues including the crop seeds which nourish humans and animals. Indeed, the protein in the 1973-1974 U.S. alfalfa crop was almost twice as much as that in the 12.5 million metric tons of soybean meal utilized in the U.S. that same year.

Process research is well developed for a commercial system which would be added to a conventional dehydration plant to recover whole leaf protein. When economic feasibility studies are completed by the U.S. Department of Agriculture, a full-scale demonstration plant will be recommended for construction at the site of a commercial dehydration plant.

Process research for an on-the-farm-type leaf protein recovery system (in connection with silage or hay production from the press cake) has been undertaken by workers at the University of Wisconsin and elsewhere. This work involves low-cost equipment development, and further research on production and quality of the silage and/or hay produced.

Research applicable to both types of systems is needed for optimization of unit operations, for higher-value utilization of the residual juice solubles fraction, and for economic analysis of the several possible variants in the systems.

Denatured white (insoluble) products are made by heat coagulation of chlorophyll-free alfalfa juice after prior removal of the green protein fraction. A great deal of further research is needed to increase yields of this white protein, to increase its purity, and to explore its utilization possibilities in various types of food.

When *Nicotiana* (tobacco) species are used as raw leaf materials, a white protein (Fraction I protein) can be obtained readily in pure crystalline form. This tasteless, pure-white product should have special value where high purity is needed. Research is needed on growing these plants on an intensive scale, on determination of the economic value of the crystalline protein, and on the economics of its production.

It may be concluded that leafy plants have tremendous potential for supplying an important proportion of the protein requirements of both monogastric animals and man by the years 1985-2000. What is needed is a coherent, well-financed, multidisciplinary research effort in the agronomic, genetic, chemical, engineering, nutritional, toxiocological, microbiological, and food technological aspects of leaf protein production.

Chemical Synthesis of Nutrients

The possibility exists of filling some of humankind's protein needs by nontraditional means, particularly by chemical synthesis. Synthetic vitamins and amino acids are, of course, already in common use. While the cost of their chemical synthesis is relatively high compared to the cost of products made by fermentation, the use of mixtures made from a common intermediate might considerably reduce the cost.

Synthesis of industrial fatty acid from carbon monoxide was conducted in wartime Germany, and increased efficiency is possible. The synthesis of glycerol for human food has also been investigated, particularly by the National Aeronautics and Space Administration, as a potential food energy source. A more advanced approach involves 1, 3-butane diol, which is metabolized with 50 percent greater energy output than are sugars or glycerol.

Recent studies have shown that normal paraffins can provide some metabolic energy to chickens. There is a strong possibility that an efficient and relatively high-yielding synthesis of ATP can be developed using HCN as a starting material for adenine. All such developments, however, are clearly in the area of long-range prospects.

Concluding Comments

The squeeze on international food supply in the early 1970's changed in the late 1970's to a renewed abundance of U.S. grain crops, at a time when production world-over had also increased.

From this, it could be argued that the research needs proposed here are no longer realistic or necessary. It should be emphasized, however, that the depressed world grain prices, which have generated significant political repercussions in the U.S., cannot prevail indefinitely. The relative plateau in U.S. consumer food costs has not retreated substantially from the peak levels of 1974 and 1975, notwithstanding the sharp drop in crop prices.

One can anticipate that when commodity prices rise to a level which will provide U.S. grain farmers with a fair return, there will be another significant increase in consumer food costs. When this happens, new or unconventional sources of protein will have greater chance of competing with traditional products, just as new energy sources will become economically feasible as the cost of traditional energy supplies continues to escalate. Research to make these developments possible, like the show in the theatre, must go on.

Restraints In Accepting New Foods: Relationships Among Taste, Acceptability, And Digestion

Joseph G. Brand, Morley R. Kare, and Michael Naim

Taste represents one basis for recognizing familiar and unfamiliar foods. The catalog of familiar (i.e., "safe") foods for humans is fairly limited. Food habits are one of the last characteristics of a cultural group to disappear as the culture changes. Under normal conditions, ventures into new foods proceed slowly and cautiously (Rozin, 1976). Factors as diverse as economics and nutritional deficiencies can, however, influence dietary choices. For example, nutritional deficits trigger exploratory food search behaviors in fowl (Wood-Gush, 1966). Thus, at some point, novelty can become more important than familiarity in food selection, in spite of the risks in sampling new foods. Even though humans are generally conservative in food habits, behavioral mechanisms exist for the acceptance of new foods. The sense of taste plays a role in these exploratory behaviors.

Taste and flavor perception are important in discriminating one food from another; taste is also involved in the decision of whether or not to ingest a food. The taste system forms an obvious gating function for food acceptance, and, as such, stands as the last sentinel to unpalatable or potentially harmful foods. While taste serves as a protector against foods of questionable quality, it also can serve a positive function in motivating ingestion. Grewal et al. (1973) report that even a highly preferred flavor (almond) did not increase the intake of a concentrated food supplement in children four to seven years old, yet adding sucrose to a 14.85 percent level significantly increased acceptance of the supplement.

To suggest that taste alone has a paramount role in determining ingestion is an obvious overextension. Tastes which are normally rejected in aqueous solution (such as bitter, sour, or highly salty) are often sought out in a "real" food or drink. Apparently, the context in which these tastes appear is crucial. This variable is difficult to evaluate quantitatively, yet it seems to be a result of experience and may parallel cognitive development. Thus, what is considered palatable in a food (and even pleasant in taste) varies greatly depending upon the context in which it is found, and the past experience and culture of the individual. All these variables together influence the decision to ingest.

[105]

Taste also acts as a trigger to initiate certain digestive processes reflexively, even before food reaches the gut (Pavlov, 1910; Nicolaidis, 1969). The nervous system pathways responsible for these reflexes are not well characterized, but probably involve gustatory-vagal interactions. Branches of the vagus (Xth cranial nerve) innervate both the oral cavity and the abdominal viscera; chemical triggers in the oral cavity could influence the functioning of this nerve in the digestive system via a relay in the brain. Learning may also influence the expression of these reflexes. So, it is possible that the actual taste quality of a food (sweet, sour, salty, or bitter) has a modulating affect on digestive function.

Taste is not the only factor that determines food acceptability; all of the other senses are involved in food selection. These include the sight of the food, the smell of the food, the textural variables of the food, and, perhaps, even the sound of the food as it is being eaten (Beauchamp and Maller, 1977; Vickers and Bourne, 1976; Szczeniak and Kahn, 1971). An animal uses all of its senses in locating, identifying, and determining palatability of a food. Ingestion of food is delicately balanced between two main forces: the need to take in food in order to fulfill nutritional requirements, and the need to reject foods which are either poisonous or nutritionally dilute. Poisons are found in the food environment, and many are associated with otherwise nutritious foods. Animals that sample a large catalog of potential foods thus require mechanisms not only for acceptance but also for rejection of food. The forces that are involved in dictating the development and modification of food acceptance and rejection mechanisms are in many cases directly related to taste.

Taste Discrimination

The basic taste qualities (dimensions) in man are usually considered as four in number: sweet, salty, sour, and bitter. While these four dimensions are generally recognized as unique, non-overlapping functions, the restriction to four qualities is not universally accepted (McBurney, 1974; Schiffman and Erickson, 1971). As first suggested by Ohrwall (1891), the basic taste qualities may be the result of four sensory systems, and not simply points on a continuum of taste modalities. Neurologically, one would then postulate that the sense of taste is based on a labelled line hypothesis, such as that originally proposed by Miller for neurological functioning. That is, neurons exist which, when fired, signal only the sensation "sweet" or only the sensation "bitter," regardless of the manner in which they are stimulated. This hypothesis was transferred to taste by von Bekesy (1966), and later supported by other psychophysical and electrophysiological work (Dzendolet, 1964; Wang, 1971). Others have presented evidence that the nervous system in taste distinguishes gustatory qualities by a pattern of fiber discharges (Erickson, 1963). It is possible that both of these mechanisms are utilized in the recognition of complex stimuli such as foods (Pfaffman, 1974).

The structure of a compound cannot be used to predict the sensation that it may elicit in an individual. While it is true that, for humans, sour is associated with a freely dissociable hydrogen ion, the anion of the acid plays a large role in the magnitude and quality of the perception of sour (Beidler, 1967). The inorganic salts of sodium generally produce a salty but complex taste. Sodium chloride is regarded as the most nearly "pure" salty taste. Lithium chloride has a taste very close to that of sodium chloride, though animals can be taught to discriminate between the two (Harriman and Kare, 1964). Other inorganic salts have a complex taste; for example, potassium chloride tastes both salty and bitter.

Studies of the chemical structure of sweet compounds have revealed some patterns which are consistent among stimuli, but this work is incomplete (Birch, 1976). Correlations between structure and the ability of a compound to elicit a bitter sensation are very complex, and no theory has emerged that can explain the structure-function relationships for these compounds. Confounding a simple structure-activity relationship is the observation that stimuli reported as sweet can be distinguished one from another on the basis of taste. For example, glucose, sucrose, saccharin, and monellin are all labeled sweet, yet individuals can distinguish among them. The vast array of chemicals that taste bitter can also generally be distinguished from one another. Perceptual subtleties such as these would imply that the reception of taste information involves a more complex relationship than that which could be provided by a single stimulus-receptor hypothesis for each of the four dimensions.

Taste and Food Preferences

Ingestion of food is partly controlled by the degree of pleasure evoked by particular tastes. Affective responses to taste stimulation are important determinants in food acceptance, and evidence to date suggests that these are controlled by both genetic factors and experience. For humans, many stimuli, most of them sweet, rise in pleasantness to a maximum, then decline with increasing concentration. While there are individual variations, in general the preference curves for sweet stimuli trace an inverted U function. Bitter and sour substances usually produce a decrease in preference with an increasing concentration. And, as might also be expected, stimuli of the same dimension often do not display exactly the same hedonic function. Individual variations are quite interesting, since these may reflect more than "noise" within the population. These may, for example, indicate differences in genetic makeup, development, or experience. Such differences might then be referable to food habits, and these to the general problem of the acceptability of new foods.

Experimental evidence does exist to suggest that responses to certain taste dimensions are innate, while other responses either develop later or are learned. Desor et al. (1973) demonstrated that human newborns prefer sugar solutions over water. The infants' preference for particular types of sugars (sucrose, glucose, fructose) corresponds with adult perception of their relative sweetness. Other data (Desor, Maller, and Andrews, 1975) on the newborn failed to demonstrate preference or aversion to salt (.05 to .2M NaCl), or to the taste of urea (.18 to .48M). This result with urea as a bitter stimulus should not be generalized to other bitter stimuli. The taste of urea is complex, having both salty and sour overtones. These investigators could not use other bitter stimuli or higher concentrations of urea because of the potential danger to the health of the infants.

Other studies examining the facial expressions of neonates after taste stimuli are placed in the oral cavity would suggest that infants find quinine aversive (Steiner, 1973). However, since no intake studies have been performed, the question of acceptance of bitter stimuli by neonates cannot be addressed. Some dislike of sour (.001 to .024M citric acid) was demonstrable when compared to the control of .07M sucrose in water (Desor, Maller, and Andrews, 1975). These studies also produced evidence that water was an aversive stimulus to the newborn.

While human newborns are apparently indifferent to the taste of sodium chloride, children of one and a half to three years of age find salt in water aversive (Beauchamp and Maller, 1977). It was suggested that, by this age, the context in which salt is presented becomes meaningful, and salty water is then rejected, whereas a salt-flavored soup (a complex liquid), or a salty snack food (solid), may be preferred. Presumably, previous intake experiences have interceded by this age to dictate acceptance and rejection based on context as well as taste.

Whether or not taste preferences remain stable after weaning is not known, since appropriate longitudinal studies have not been performed. Some cross-sectional studies have, however, been completed and their data are relevant to this question. One study (Desor, Greene, and Maller, 1975) determined taste preference levels of nine to fifteen year olds and adults for several concentrations of sucrose, lactose, and sodium chloride. The results indicate that the preference levels are not the same for adolescents and adults. Adults preferred less concentrated solutions of these three stimuli than did adolescents. Since this was not a longitudinal study, it is impossible to say whether these shifting preferences are a result of maturation or are a product of different food experiences for the two age groups. The responses to sugar could be related to the variable calorie needs of the two populations.

Evidence exists which demonstrates that an individual's sensitivity to one class of bitter compounds, the thioureas, is under genetic control (Kalmus, 1971). The most commonly used taste stimulus in this chemical class is phenythiourea (PTC). In a given population, individuals are either sensitive to ("tasters") or relatively insensitive to ("non-tasters") the bitter taste of PTC. This taste dimorphism has been exploited in many anthropological and genetic studies (Bonné et al., 1972; Scott-Emaukpur et al., 1975; Greene, 1974). Many of the thioureas are goitrogenic. One report (Greene, 1974) suggests that the ability of an individual to taste these compounds in food, in a region of Ecuador where goiter is endemic, may serve a protective function by limiting the consumption of these goitrogenic foods.

The acceptance of the taste of a sweet compound is immediate even in individuals who have never before been exposed to this sensation. Thus, this preference for the sweet modality may be innate. Likewise, the selection for sodium via a taste mechanism is immediate when the animal is under a sodium deficit. This recognition of sodium by taste argues for the innateness of the salt response (Nachman and Cole, 1971). However, Greene et al. (1975) found that heritability estimates for *preferences* of particular levels of sucrose, lactose, and sodium chloride were zero. The possibility that early intake experience plays a role in dictating the level of taste preference should be considered.

Moskowitz et al. (1975) reported that laborers in India rate citric acid increasingly pleasant with concentration and quinine sulfate pleasant at low concentrations. This pattern was not observed in another group of individuals, Indian medical students, who exhibited what would be considered classical aversions for these stimuli. The laborers' diet was marked by particularly large quantities of sour foods, while that of the students was traditional Western cuisine. The relative health of the two populations is an uncontrollable confounding factor. For example, calorie deficits can influence food palatability, and apparently the general metabolic state of the animal feeds back to the functioning of the peripheral taste receptors (Sharma et al., 1977). Even though the nutritional state of an animal can apparently influence the functioning of a sensory system, the data for the Moskowitz study is compelling. It suggests that food intake experience can influence simple taste preference.

In summary, the data from taste testing indicates that, in humans, the preference for sweet is innate. Relative preferences for salty, bitter, and sour may change with age due to experiential or developmental processes. Preferences for all tastes can be influenced by context, and the degree to which a particular taste is preferred may be under experiential control. The data of Moskowitz et al. (1975) suggest that previous food experience does influence taste preferences, and that experience presumably would be a major determinant to the acceptability of a unique food or flavor.

Taste and the Assessment of Food Quality

The role that taste plays in food selection and ingestion is complicated and has received only minimal attention. Acceptable food quality for an animal falls within a fairly narrow range. An animal apparently depends on at least two mechanisms to insure that any ingested food will not be poisonous. First, there are learning mechanisms which use taste (flavor) as a cue, so that any deleterious postingestion consequences can be associated with a food previously eaten. Since most feral animals that have been tested generally display an aversion to new foods, their slow acceptance of novel foods usually assures them of enough time to make this type of quality assessment. When presented with a new food source, the animal samples it without ingesting a large quantity of it. If the new source has a unique flavor, the animal apparently retains the memory of that flavor when categorizing this source as novel. If deleterious effects follow this sampling, the food is no longer eaten. Only the flavor of the diet is paired with consequences, regardless of intervening variables. This type of learning about foods has been termed "conditioned taste (or food) aversion" and has received considerable attention (Rozin and Kalat, 1971; Garcia et al., 1974).

An animal can also make quality assessments of food based on taste alone. The relative acceptability of taste stimuli can be determined using a simple two-choice preference test, although any one chemical stimulus will not elicit the same behavior from all animals. When given a choice of two foods (one adulterated with a chemical shown to be aversive to that animal, the other unadulterated), animals show a general preference for the unadulterated or, presumably, more palatable food. The aversive taste may have more than a hedonic component, since many aversive stimuli are poisons. Most of these are rejected both in two-choice liquid tests and two-choice solid diet experiments. However, an animal generalizes from this strict interpretation only to its peril, since many essential nutrients, such as some amino acids, are bitter to humans and may be aversive to other animals.

One recent experiment illustrates the role of taste in food selection, and suggests that mechanisms exist which can override its dictates. Figure 10.1 illustrates an experiment wherein rats made a choice between two diets differing not only in taste, but also in nutritional potential (Naim et al., 1977). One diet contained defatted raw soybeans as a protein source, with the addition of 0.35 percent (w/w) sodium saccharin (appealing taste); the other diet contained defatted heated soybeans, with the addition of the aversive tasting substance sucrose octaacetate (2.0 percent, w/w). Raw soybeans have a lower nutritional value than heated or cooked soybeans, primarily because the raw form contains digestive enzyme inhibitors and other thermolabile factors which give rise to undesirable physiological consequences. Given a choice between these two diets over a period of 14 days, the animals initially preferred the diet with the appealing taste (figure 10.1A). However, after six to seven days, the animals changed preference to the diet with better nutrition but poorer taste. When quinine sulfate was substituted for sucrose octaacetate in the above regimen, the animals never

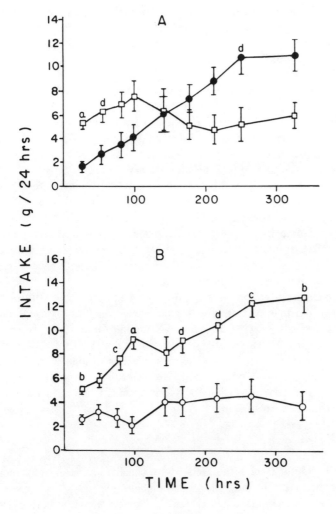

Fig. 10.1

displayed a preference for the diet with better nutrition but poorer taste (figure 10.1B).

The change in preference in the first experiment may be explained by assuming that postingestional factors influenced the animals to eventually choose the diet offering better nutrition, even though it contained an aversive taste substance. Additionally, the raw soy diet may have contained other offensive flavors that eventually became paired with negative postingestional factors. Thus, the separation in preference between the two diets in part A of figure 10.1 may be a result of more than one taste—postingestional pairing. This change in preference was not evident when quinine was substituted for sucrose octaacetate. Quinine has known adverse pharmacological activity, whereas sucrose octaacetate is relatively harmless. Apparently, the animals were able to gauge this pharmacological activity through some systemic mechanism. Thus, despite the better nutrition afforded by that food, the rats avoided the quinine-adulterated diet. Since no pharmacological effect was evident from the sucrose octaacetate-adulterated diet, the initial "distrust" of this diet affording better nutrition was overcome, and a strong preference followed. The animals, however, were very conservative in making this change, allowing six to seven days for assessment. The influence of taste in dictating diet preference is thus displayed.

In a no-choice situation, where growing rats are presented with only one diet, either flavored or not, aversive taste cues will not change total diet consumed nor efficiency of utilization (Naim and Kare, 1977); Naim, Kare, and Ingle, 1978). However, at least with rats, the pattern of eating changes beyond a certain point. As the diet is made less palatable, meal size and intermeal intervals increase (Gentile, 1970). Since the animal is literally eating to survive, the taste problems take on secondary importance, yet still influence some aspects of eating.

Taste and Food Digestion

While the role of taste in food selection is usually obvious, less appreciated are the effects that taste and oral stimulation have on the systemic physiology of the organism. This phenomenon was first demonstrated by Pavlov (1910), yet has received only minimal attention since then. Oral stimulation can modify not only the metabolic reflexes as measured by Nicolaidis (1969, 1977), but also intestinal motility and the secretory processes along the gastrointestinal tract. Pavlov, for example, demonstrated that chewing of palatable substances by dogs initiated gastric secretions. Little effect was noted for neutral-tasting substances. Taste is only one of several cues that operate in the cephalic phase of gastric secretion. Other stimuli besides taste are the thought, expectation, sight, smell, chewing, and swallowing of food. The cephalic phase of gastric secretion is mediated by the vagus nerve. These gastric secretory responses appear five to seven minutes after sham-feeding and may continue as copious secretions for as long as three hours (Brooks, 1967). Humans have been shown to demonstrate this response as well (Knutson and Olbe, 1971). In humans, it has been suggested that when all phases (i.e., cephalic, gastric, and intestinal) are operating simultaneously, the cephalic phase is responsible for one-third of the total amount of gastric acid secretion (Richardson et al, 1977).

In addition to gastric secretions, pancreatic exocrine secretions can also be influenced by the cephalic phase in general, and by taste in particular. Pancreatic flow rate and protein output increase in dogs following sham feeding (Preshaw et al, 1966). The use of appropriate controls led to the conclusion that this effect could not be attributed to a secondary stimulus such as the passage of gastric contents into the intestine. The magnitude of this orally triggered pancreatic release is unknown. The pancreas has vagal innervation, and there is evidence for direct neural stimulation of pancreatic secretion (Crittenden and Ivy, 1937). However, such a mechanism is probably unimportant compared with the vagally mediated release of the hormone gastrin (Preshaw et al, 1966). Yet both mechanisms are operable and, perhaps, both are normally required for optimal pancreatic function.

Little consideration has been given to the effect that actual taste stimuli may have on pancreatic output. Studies by Behrman and Kare (1968) showed that the taste of a diet could modulate pancreatic flow and protein content in conscious dogs fitted with a duodenal fistula (for cannulation of the pancreatic duct) and a gastric fistula (for emptying the stomach). Water and sucrose mixed with the basal diet produced greater flow and protein output than did citric acid or quinine mixed with the diet. Yet the role of taste alone, as well as the role of other eating functions (tongue movements, mastication, swallowing), were not separated.

Other experiments have since attempted to segregate some of these possible sources of pancreatic reflexive activity (Naim and Kare, 1977; Naim, Kare, and Merritt, 1978). To check the effect of taste alone, conscious dogs with Thomas gastric and duodenal fistulas were stimulated by swab application of taste solutions. While sucrose was a better stimulant than either citric acid or quinine, the secretory response was extinguished after only one or two trials with each stimulant. Apparently, the animals rapidly adapted to this test situation, and when food was not forthcoming after stimulation, pancreatic output was inhibited. When the same dogs were presented a taste stimulus mixed in cellulose, and permitted to chew and swallow the mixture, they showed gradually increasing pancreatic secretion. Flow and protein content increased more for the sucrose-cellulose mixture than for citric acid, quinine, or deionized water (control)-cellulose mixtures. Figure 10.2 details the protein output of pancreatic exocrine secretions under these conditions. Measures of volume output generally paralleled protein output. These results

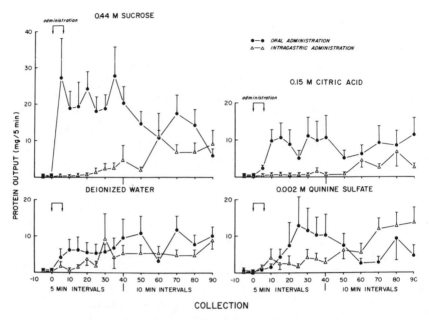

COLLECTION

Fig. 10.2

demonstrate that taste alone is not a sufficient stimulus for pancreatic secretion, but coupled with normal eating patterns, can modulate both pancreatic flow and protein output.

Taste, as well as oral stimulation in general, can trigger an immediate rise in circulating levels of insulin. It has been demonstrated that orally administered glucose results in higher blood levels of immunoreactive insulin (IRI) than levels obtained when similar levels of blood glucose are produced by intravenous infusions (Elrick et al., 1964). Also, the hormones functioning in exocrine pancreatic regulation (secretin, gastrin, and choleocystokinin) can cause an increase in insulin in the pancreaticoduodenal venous plasma after their rapid endoportal injection in anesthetized dogs (Unger et al., 1967). Insulin secretion during oral feeding occurs in at least two stages. The first stage is triggered only by oral stimulation, and can occur without changes in blood glucose levels. The phases following this initial one are the results of foods and fluids acting in the gut before absorption, and of circulating nutrients acting after absorption (Fischer et al., 1972; Steffens, 1976). Steffens has shown (1976) that the initial IRI peak is entirely dependent on oral stimulation and occurs within one minute of stimulation. Gastric infusion of food also leads to a rise in IRI, but only after three minutes. This latter IRI rise parallels blood glucose increases. Fischer et al. (1972) have shown that after mucosal anaesthesia of the oral cavity, this immediate IRI increase is absent.

Experiments point to other systemic functions besides the secretion of enzymes that can be affected by oral stimulation. Nicolaidis (1969, 1977) has, for example, demonstrated oral metabolic reflexes in:
1) respiratory quotient measurements in response to eating;
2) hyperglycemic responses to oral stimulation with saccharin or sucrose in hungry rats;
3) an almost immediate increased sweating by dehydrated human subjects in a hot room when fluids are consumed; and
4) an increase in diuresis by stimulation of the mouth of a rat with water. Stimulation of the oral cavity with 5 percent NaCl resulted in inhibition of diuresis. An immediate inhibition of diuresis is also reportedly produced by eating solid foods (Kakolewski and Valenstein, 1969).

All of these metabolic effects are anticipatory, since they precede and are in the same direction as the changes which are produced by the foods as a result of digestive and post-absorptive systemic influences. These gustatory-metabolic reflexes promote the efficient digestion of food and would seem to guarantee the already over-optimized digestive processes.

Thus, while taste and oral stimulation have demonstrable effects on the systemic physiology of the organism, questions remain as to whether these play a nutritionally relevant role in food utilization. An aversive stimulus such as sucrose octaacetate or quinine sulfate, when added to the diet of a weanling rat, did not affect total daily food intake or growth efficiency (Naim and Kare, 1977; Naim, Kare, and Ingle, 1978). It is therefore possible that gastrointestinal and pancreatic functioning are not affected severely enough by these aversive tastes to change food digestion efficiency. Mechanisms which control food digestion may be overoptimally set. For example, digestive enzymes may be present in concentrations beyond the normal needs of the system. Also, the animal may rapidly habituate to the aversive taste, so that any affects of food taste on digestive functions may not be overtly demonstrable. It should be possible, however, to interfere with such habituation by regularly changing the taste of the diet with randomly selected stimuli. When this was performed on a daily basis (Naim, Kare, and Ingle, 1977), the results were quite dramatic. Rats fed a diet which was adequate except for an aversive taste stimulus whose character was changed daily showed a 25 percent inhibition in growth efficiency over a six day period, and a 15 percent inhibition after eighteen days. Surprisingly, total food intake was not different between experimental and control animals (Table 10.1). Pharmacological effects of the taste stimuli were ruled out. Thus, daily changes in the taste of the diet may have interfered, through cephalic mechanisms, with digestive or metabolic processes. For example, changing the taste of the diet could be a sufficient physiological stress to influence the pituitary-adrenal system. If so, a release of ACTH could have enhanced the catabolic processes of the animals and resulted in the observed

TABLE 10.1

THE EFFECT OF AVERSIVE STIMULI[a] ON FOOD INTAKE AND GROWTH EFFICIENCY IN WEANLING RATS

Addition[a] To The 10% Protein (Casein) diet	Days After Start of Experiment					
	6		11		18	
	Total Food Intake[b]	Growth Efficiency[b]	Total Food Intake	Growth Efficiency	Total Food Intake	Growth Efficiency
None (control)	52 ± 3[c]	0.40 ± 0.02	111 ± 4	0.40 ± 0.02	202 ± 8	0.35 ± 0.01
SOA	51 ± 2	0.35 ± 0.02	106 ± 5	0.38 ± 0.01	194 ± 8	0.34 ± 0.01
SOA, QS, CA or Sacc.	50 ± 3	0.30*± 0.02	104 ± 5	0.35*± 0.02	196 ± 9	0.30*± 0.01

a. The aversive stimuli were sucrose octaacetate (SOA), quinine sulfate (QS), citric acid (CA) and saccharin (Sacc) to 3.0%, 0.04%, 3.0%, and 2.5% (w/w) of the diet. A daily change to a different aversive taste stimulus occurred in a predetermined order. An amount of cornstarch equivalent to the added weight of the aversive stimulus was removed for each diet.

b. Total food intake is calculated as the total grams of food eaten per rat. Growth efficiency is calculated as the gram body weight gain per gram of food intake.

c. Values are cumulative mean ± SEM of 13 rats per group.

*Significantly lower values (P<0.05) than the corresponding controls fed the unadulterated casein diet.

inhibition of growth. It must therefore be concluded that changing the taste of a complete diet on a daily basis is sufficient to markedly affect growth and nutritional well-being of rats.

The Modification of Basic Tastes

Since taste is known to be at least one of the possible limitations to food acceptance, the natural question to ask is: Can taste be modified? To certain extents, the taste of foods or beverages can be either changed by, for example, loading the food with a single dominant taste such as sweet or salty, or can be enhanced through the use of known flavor enhancers such as monosodium glutamate. The results of these approaches are largely predictable from food technology, provided one is using a well known food base. But their application to new foods, such as those with unique flavors or textures, is not known. Careful experimentation with additives and flavor enhancers would appear to be the only way to determine the effect of these on each new food analog.

There is another aspect to modifying the taste of food which is not always appreciated in food technology. Rather than modifying the food itself, one might also consider the modification of the taste receptors. Monosodium glutamate probably works in this way, although its exact mode of action and the mechanism of the synergism between it and the ribonucleotides is unknown. Certain speculations, however, have been made (Cagan, 1977). Other chemicals are known to either block a specific taste or to cause one modality to be perceived as another. It is generally agreed that these effects are brought about at the level of the taste bud.

The sweet antagonist, gymnemic acid, suppresses the sensation of sweet after a solution of it is placed in the mouth (Kurihara, 1971). Gymnemic acid is isolated from the leaves of the plant *Gymnema sylvestre*. It appears as a glycoside with glucoronic acid. Several structural analogs are known. Prewashing the tongue with a solution of gymnemic acid or simply chewing the leaves of the plant abolishes the sweetness normally perceived from such compounds as sucrose, glucose, saccharin, or the sweet protein monellin. Its antagonism is specific for the sweet modality. One might assume, therefore, that it simply inhibits the binding of the sweet stimuli to their receptor sites. However, a direct test of this hypothesis showed, at least at the level of analysis possible at that time, that no inhibition of 14C-sucrose binding to taste bud and control tissue homogenates was evident (Cagan, 1974). An increasingly prevalent hypothesis in taste physiology states that there is more than one unique receptor site for sweet. One report delineates four such sites (Faurion, 1977). Yet gymnemic acid inhibits the sweetness evident from all sweet stimuli, regardless of probable receptor site. This fact, plus the negative data on binding competition, suggests that gymnemic acid exerts its antagonistic effect at a step subsequent to binding, possibly a major transductive step. Yet it acts only as a sweet antagonist, and has no activity on the other three modalities. Thus for this hypothesis to be viable, one must also assume that at least part of the transductive path for the sensation "sweet" is unique.

Another taste modifier, miraculin or miracle fruit (Kurihara, 1971), is a glycoprotein of molecular weight about 44,000. It is isolated from the fruit of the tropical plant *Synsepalum dulcificum* and is a true modifier, in that prewashing the tongue with a solution of the protein permits the changing of one quality, sour, to another quality, sweet. This protein itself has no inherent taste. The modifying effect persists for a period of time which is dependent on the concentration of the protein initially used, from a few minutes to hours. The sweetness induced by a particular acid is related to the intensity of sourness of that acid. Gymnemic acid can inhibit the sweetness induced by this protein. Kurihara et al. (1969) suggest that the protein acts by inserting its arabinose or xylose moiety into a sweet receptor site after the sour substance has changed the conformation of the receptor plasma membrane.

It has been reported that analogs in the sweetener class dihydrochalcones interfere with the bitterness of narrigin and limonin (Guadagni et al., 1974). The thresholds of these latter two bitter stimuli were increased by pre-washing the mouth with the chalcone derivatives. In view of the fact that bitterness almost always plagues new food formulations, this is a particularly interesting finding.

In principle, it is possible to use group-specific protein reagents to inhibit the receptive function of proteins. Early reports suggested that some specificity toward modalities was possible by selecting the appropriate reagents (Yureva, 1961; Noma and Hiji, 1972). However, these results were subsequently challenged by Mooser (1976) and Mooser and Lambuth (1977). They provide evidence that reagents blocking sulfhydryl function (analogs of n-ethyl maleimide), as well as those blocking carbonyl functionalities, exert their antagonistic effects by inhibiting transduction of sweet, sour, and salty chemical messages. It is possible that additional experimentation may uncover blocking reagents that will be specific toward particular modalities, but none have been confirmed.

Concluding Remarks

The necessity for the discovery, formulation, and production of foods not previously found in human culinary experience is evident. Do studies to date on taste and acceptance provide any guidelines for formulations of the taste of these new foods? In other words, should we imitate or innovate? We now appreciate the conservatism of cuisine and are aware of the acceptability of traditional tastes and flavors within a cultural group. We would need to conclude from those studies that imitation of existing flavors is preferable to innovation. Yet experience tells us that innovation in the production of new foods or beverages is not to be overlooked. The overwhelming acceptance of cola beverages is an obvious example. Of course, the acceptance of a beverage, and a snack beverage at that, may have little relevance to the probable acceptance of a new food item that is designed to imitate a food of central importance to the culture's cuisine. Thus, if a new food is to be introduced into a culture, it may be necessary to design it as a food of peripheral importance to the cuisine, such as a snack-type item. It would appear prudent, therefore, to imitate only if this can be done more or less exactly, and to innovate with the aim of introducing not a variant of a staple food, but an entirely new food.

Acknowledgement

The authors thank Drs. G. Beauchamp and C.M. Christensen for their critical appraisal of the manuscript.

References

Beauchamp, G. K., and O. Maller
  1977   The development of flavor preferences in humans: a review. In *The Chemical Senses and Nutrition*, M. R. Kare and O. Maller, eds., Academic Press, New York, p. 291.

Behrman, H. R., and M. R. Kare
  1968   Canine pancreatic secretion in response to acceptable and aversive taste stimuli. *Proceedings of the Society for Experimental Biology and Medicine 129*:343.

Beidler, L. M.
  1967   Anion influences on taste receptor response. In *Olfaction and Taste II*, T. Hayashi, ed., Pergamon Press, New York, p. 509.

Bekesy, G. von
  1966   Taste theories and the chemical stimulation of single papillae. *Journal of Applied Physiology 21*:1.

Birch, G. G.
  1976   Structural relationships of sugars to taste. *CRC Critical Reviews in Food Science and Nutrition*, September, p. 57.

Bonné, B., S. Ashbel, G. Berlin, and B. Sela
  1972   The Habbanite isolate III. Anthropometrics, taste sensitivity, and color vision. *Human Heredity 22*:430.

Brooks, F. P.
  1967   Central neural control of acid secretion. In *Handbook of Physiology*, Vol. 2, C. F. Code, ed., American Physiological Association, Washington, D.C., p. 805.

Cagan, R. H.
  1974   Biochemistry of sweet sensation. In *Sugars in Nutrition*, H. L. Sipple and K. W. McNutt, eds., Academic Press, New York, p. 19.

Cagan, R. H.
1977   A framework for the mechanisms of action of special taste substances:
            The example of monosodium glutamate. In *The Chemical Senses and
            Nutrition*, M. R. Kare and O. Maller, eds., Academic Press, New York,
            p. 343.

Crittenden, P. J. and A. C. Ivy
1937   The nervous control of pancreatic secretion in the dog. *American
            Journal of Physiology 119:*724.

Desor, J. A., L. S. Greene, and O. Maller
1975   Preferences for sweet and salty in 9- to 15-year-old and adult humans.
            Science 190:686.

Desor, J. A., O. Maller, and K. Andrews
1975   Ingestive responses of human newborns to salty, sour, and bitter
            stimuli. *Journal of Comparative and Physiological Psychology 89*:966.

Desor, J. A., O. Maller, and R. Turner
1973   Taste in acceptance of sugars by human infants. *Journal of Comparative
            and Physiological Psychology 84*:496.

Dzendolet, E.
1964   Basis for taste quality in man. In *Olfaction and Taste III*, C. Pfaffmann,
            ed., Rockefeller University Press, New York, p. 420.

Elrick, H., L. Stimmler, C. J. Lad, and Y. Arai
1964   Plasma insulin response to oral and intravenous glucose administration.
            Journal of Clinical Endocrinology and Metabolism 24:1076.

Erickson, R. P.
1963   Sensory neural patterns and gustation. In *Olfaction and Taste I*, Y.
            Zotterman, ed., Pergamon Press, Oxford, p. 205.

Faurion, A., S. Saito, and P. MacLeod
1977   Abstract to the Sixth International Symposium on Olfaction and Taste,
            Paris, France, July, 1977.

Fischer, U., H. Hommel, M. Ziegler, and E. Jutzi
1972   The mechanism of insulin secretion after oral glucose administration:
            II. Investigations on the mechanism of a reflectoric insulin mobilization
            after oral stimulation. *Diabetologia 8:*385.

Fischer, U., H. Hommel, M. Ziegler, and R. Michael
1972   The mechanism of insulin secretion after oral glucose administration: I.
            Multiphasic source of insulin mobilization after oral administration of
            glucose in conscious dogs. *Diabetologia 8*:104.

Garcia, J., W. G. Hankins, and K. W. Rusiniak
1974   Behavioral regulation of the milieu interne in man and rat. *Science
            185:*824.

Gentile, R. L.
1970   The role of taste preference in the eating behavior of the albino rat.
            Physiology and Behavior 5:311.

Greene, L. S.
1974   Physical growth and development, neurological maturation, and
            behavioral functioning in communities in which goiter is endemic. II.
            PTC taste sensitivity and neurological maturation. *American Journal of
            Physical Anthropology 41:*139.

Greene, L. S., J. A. Desor, and O. Maller
1975   Heredity and experience: Their relative importance in the development
            of taste preference in man. *Journal of Comparative and Physiological
            Psychology 89:*279.

Grewal, T., T. Gopaldas, P. Hartenberger, I. Ramakrishnan, and G. Ramachandran
1973   *Journal of Food Science and Technology 10*:149.

Guadagni, D. G., V. P. Maier, and J. G. Turnbaugh
  1974   Some factors affecting sensory threshholds and relative bitterness of
            limonin and naringin. *Journal of the Science of Food and Agriculture*
            25:1199.

Harriman, A. E., and M. R. Kare
  1964   Preference for sodium chloride over lithium chloride by
            adrenalectomized rats. *American Journal of Physiology 207:*941.

Kakolewski, J. W., and E. S. Valenstein
  1969   Antidiuresis associated with the ingestion of food substances. In
            Olfaction and Taste III, C. Pfaffmann, ed., Rockefeller University Press,
            New York, p. 593.

Kalmus, H.
  1971   Genetics of taste. Chapter 9 in *Handbook of Sensory Physiology,* Vol.
            IV, part 2, L. M. Beidler, ed., Springer-Verlag, New York, p. 165.

Knutson, U., and L. Olbe
  1971   In *Gastrointestinal Hormones and Other Subjects,* E. H. Thaysen, ed.,
            Munksgaard, Copenhagen, p. 25.

Kurihara, K.
  1971   Taste Modifiers. Chapter 16 in *Handbook of Sensory Physiology,* Vol.
            IV, part 2, L. M. Beidler, ed., Springer-Verlag, New York, p. 363.

Kurihara, K., Y. Kurihara, and L. M. Beidler
  1969   Isolation and mechanism of taste modifiers; taste modifying protein
            and gymnemic acids. In *Olfaction and Taste III,* C. Pfaffmann, ed.,
            Rockefeller University Press, New York, p. 450.

McBurney, D. H.
  1974   *Chemical Senses and Flavor 1:*17.

Mooser, G.
  1976   N-substituted maleimide inactivation of the response to taste cell
            stimulation. *Journal of Neurobiology 7:*457.

Mooser, G., and N. Lambuth
  1977   Inactivation of taste receptor cell function by two cationic protein
            modification reagents. *Journal of Neurobiology 8:*193.

Moskowitz, H. W., V. Kumaraiah, K. N. Sharma, H. L. Jacobs, and S. D. Sharma
  1975   Cross-cultural differences in simple taste preferences. *Science
            190:*1217.

Nachman, M., and L. P. Cole
  1971   Role of taste in specific hungers. Chapter 15 in *Handbook of Sensory
            Physiology,* Vol. IV, part 2, L. M. Beidler, ed., Springer-Verlag, New
            York, p. 337.

Naim, M., and M. R. Kare
  1977   Taste stimuli and pancreatic functions. In *The Chemical Senses and
            Nutrition,* M. R. Kare and O. Maller, eds., Academic Press, New York,
            p. 145.

Naim, M., M. R. Kare, and D. E. Ingle
  1977   Sensory factors which affect the acceptance of raw and heated defatted
            soybeans in rats. *Journal of Nutrition 107:*1653.

Naim, M., M. R. Kare, and D. E. Ingle
  1978   Diet palatability and growth efficiency: evidence for a physiological
            interrelationship in rats. *Life Sciences 23:*2127.

Naim, M., M. R. Kare, and A. M. Merritt
  1978   Effects of oral stimulation on the cephalic phase of pancreatic exocrine
            secretion in dogs. *Physiology and Behavior 20:*563.

Noma, A., and Y. Hiji
  1972   Effects of chemical modifiers on taste responses in the rat chorda
            tympani. *Japanese Journal of Physiology 22:*393.

Nicolaidis, S.
1969   Early systemic responses to orogastric stimulation in the regulation of
            food and water balance: Functional and electrophysiological data.
            *Annals of the New York Academy of Science 157:*1176.

Nicolaidis, S.
1977   Sensory-neuroendocrine reflexes and their anticipatory and optimizing
            role on metabolism. In *The Chemical Senses and Nutrition,* M. R. Kare
            and O. Maller, eds., Academic Press, New York, p. 123.

Ohrwall, H.
1891   *Skandnavisches ouchinful physiologie.*

Pavlov, I. P.
1910   *The Work of the Digestive Glands,* 2nd edition (trans. by W. H.
            Thompson), Charles Griffin Co., Ltd., London.

Pfaffman, C.
1974   *Chemical Senses and Flavor 1:*5.

Preshaw, R. M., A. R. Cooke, and M. I. Grossman
1966   Sham feeding and pancreatic secretion in the dog. *Gastroenterology
            50:*171.

Richardson, C. T., J. H. Walsh, K. A. Cooper, M. Feldman, and J. S. Fordtran
1977   Studies on the role of cephalic-vagal stimulation in the acid secretory
            response to eating in normal human subjects. *Journal of Clinical
            Investigation 60:*435.

Rozin, P.
1976   The selection of foods by rats, humans, and other animals. In *Advances
            in the Study of Behavior* Vol. 6, J. S. Rosenblatt, R. A. Hinde, E. Shaw,
            and C. Beer, eds., Academic Press, New York, p. 21.

Rozin, P., and J. Kalat
1971   Specific hungers and poison avoidance as adaptive specializations of
            learning. *Psychological Review 78:*459.

Schiffman, S. S., and R. P. Erickson
1971   A psychophysical model for gustatory quality. *Physiology and Behavior
            7:*617.

Scott-Emaukpur, A. B., J. E. Uviovo, and S. T. Warren
1975   Genetic variation in Nigeria. I. The genetics of phenylthiourea tasting
            ability. *Human Heredity 25:*360.

Sharma, K. N., H. L. Jacobs, V. Gopal, and S. Dua-Sharma
1977   Nutritional state/taste interactions in food intake: Behavioral and
            physiological evidence for gastric/taste modulation. In *The Chemical
            Senses and Nutrition,* M. R. Kare and O. Maller, eds., Academic Press,
            New York, p. 167.

Steffens, A. B.
1976   Influence of the oral cavity on insulin release in the rat. *American
            Journal of Physiology 230:*1411.

Steiner, J. E.
1973   The gustofacial response: Observation on normal and anencephalic
            newborn infants. In *Oral Sensation and Perception,* 4th Symposium, J.
            F. Bosma, ed., Dept. of Health, Education, and Welfare, NIH, Bethesda,
            Md., p. 254.

Szczeniak, A. S., and E. L. Kahn
1971   *Journal of Texture Studies 2:*280.

Unger, R. H., H. Ketterer, J. Dupre, and A. M. Eisentraut
1967   The effects of secretin, pancreazymin, and gastrin on insulin and
            glucagon secretion in anesthetized dogs. *Journal of Clinical
            Investigation 46:*630.

Vickers, Z., and M. C. Bourne
　1976　　A psychoacoustical theory of crispness. *Journal of Food Science* 41:1158.

Wang, M. B.
　1971　　In *Research in Physiology*, F. F. Kau, K. Koizurmi, and M. Vassalle, eds., Aulo Gaggi, Bologna, p. 483.

Wood-Gush, D. G. M., and M. R. Kare
　1966　　The behavior of calcium-deficient chickens. *British Poultry Science* 7: 285.

Yureva, G. Yu
　1961　　New data on the role of protein sulfhydryl groups in taste sensitivity. *Biophysics* (USSR) 6, 2:29.

Human Adaptability
To Nutritional Stress

William A. Stini

The distinction between "adaptability" and "adaptation" is one which identifies fundamental differences in strategies of survival (Stini, 1975).

Much of the human system for coping with stress involves reversible alterations in one or more attributes. This strategy is significant because it permits the use of a variety of tactics to enhance survival within the life span of a single individual. This adaptability thus conveys to the human species the ability to confront a variety of environmental challenges, and, in a very real sense, the species has employed it to broaden its ecological niche rather than specialize for a particular habitat. The range of responses available to permit survival, known as "adaptability," stands in contrast to the genetically encoded responses referred to as "adaptation."

Species that rely upon genetic adaptations as the primary means of dealing with new challenges from the environment must necessarily do so through the action of natural selection. "Survival of the fit" often means "survival of the few" when severe habitat alterations occur. In circumstances where individual survival is of minimal significance to the strategy of species survival, population turnover is rapid. A short life span is advantageous to a species which must adapt genetically to environmental changes. Conversely, emphasis on survival of individuals has the concomitant of greater longevity (Wilson and Bossert, 1971). Greater longevity for the individual, in a world of limited resources, demands a means for limiting reproduction. Important human characteristics such as late onset of reproductive life, predominance of single births, prolonged care of offspring, and social sanctions governing interpersonal behavior, are all appropriate attributes of a species for which the predominant adaptive strategy is adaptability rather than adaptation (Slobodkin, 1968).

It is a significant fact that humans begin to reproduce much later than other animals. Even our closest relatives, the great apes, attain sexual maturity in one half to two thirds the time it takes the young human. Moreover, the human female normally ends her reproductive life long before death. Currently, in the United States, a woman's reproductive life represents only about 30 years of her life expectancy of 74+ years. Limitations on her reproductive capacity severely limit the number of offspring she will bear during those 30 years. The emphasis in human reproduction is quite clearly on survival of the relatively few offspring this system produces. This has been viewed by some as the emphasis on "quality" over "quantity."

The evolutionary history of each species is unique. One approach to an improved understanding of human biology is through the examination of the tactics facilitating the overall strategy of survival for Homo sapiens. One such tactic is nutritional. It is often referred to as the quality of "omnivorousness." Although something of an overstatement (we are physiologically incapable, for instance, of exploiting the nutritional potential of cellulose), this quality is one which influences many other aspects of human biology in many ways. While permitting the exploitation of a wide variety of food sources, characterizing a variety of habitats encompassing virtually the entire planet Earth, human omnivorousness also imposes limitations. These limitations, generally stated in terms of "minimum daily requirements," are a measure of the demands contemporary human populations make on their environment. At the same time, human nutritional requirements, and the alternative methods of satisfying them, are important clues to the nature of human adaptability and its evolutionary history.

Human Nutritional Requirements in Evolutionary Perspective

Fossil remains of extinct primates have been dated as far back as the Oligocene Epoch of the Tertiary Period, perhaps 35 million years before the present. The oldest remains resemble contemporary species collectively referred to as prosimians. It is generally thought that these prosimian-like early primates descended from some of the most primitive of early mammals, the tree-dwelling, insect-eating *Insectivora,* which probably date back to the Late Mesozoic Era, or as much as 100 million years ago.

These prosimian-like animals shared with the contemporary prosimians certain anatomical characteristics, particularly dentition, indicating adaptations to a specialized diet largely consisting of insects. Other traits associated with tree-living habits also resembled those of contemporary forms. These resemblances form an adaptive complex which may be used, albeit cautiously, to make inferences concerning the behavior of some of the earliest ancestors of our own species. Caution is necessary, of course, since we lack any samples of soft tissue which might confirm or refute allegations of dietary preference.

If contemporary prosimians are used as a model for reconstructing the dietary habits of the late Mesozoic-Early Tertiary primates, what emerges is an insectivore which may have supplemented its diet with occasional meals of vertebrate tissue and fruits in season. If this model is an accurate one, the nutritional requirements of these remote ancestors resemble our own to a greater extent than those of our closest living relatives, the great apes.

The living great apes, along with other contemporary *Anthropoidea,* rely to a large extent on vegetable sources to satisfy their nutritional requirements. It is quite certain that even the herbivorous great apes are capable of exploiting vertebrate tissues as a nutrient source when the opportunity arises, but humans are by far the largest and most frequent consumers of vertebrate tissue among the living *Hominoidea*. What is perhaps most interesting about human dietary requirements is the range of variation in nutritional patterns by which they are satisfied. While there may be similar tolerance to varied foods among other living primates, such variation is not often exploited in their natural habitats.

Judging from the fossil evidence, and that gained through observation of living primates, the logical conclusion is that the dietary habits of our own ancestors have been essentially omnivorous for perhaps 100 million years. Thus, the requirements of contemporary humans, including the essential amino acids, fatty acids, minerals, and vitamins, probably reflect a long evolutionary history during which these nutrients were available in sufficient quantities to make their synthesis unnecessary. We must obtain nine of the amino acids from food sources during the early years of life, and eight in adulthood. This is strong evidence that insect or vertebrate tissue are always available in our ancestral habitat. Our lack of means to synthesize vitamin C (shared with the other primates and guinea pigs) indicates that vegetable resources were also available.

Dietary Versatility Among Contemporary Humans

Turning to contemporary human populations, we find an array of food habits running the gamut from *almost* total carnivory to *almost* total vegetarianism. Among Eskimo, meat consumption of more than 10 kilograms per capita per day has been documented (Sinclair, 1953). Among Southeast Asian agriculturists, meat, eggs, milk, and fish are only rarely consumed and even then only in miniscule quantities. Between these extremes may be found populations whose staple foods are manioc, sweet potatoes, bananas (more properly, plantains), various grains, milk and blood, reindeer flesh, insect grubs, and a host of other animal and vegetable substances. Seemingly, the list of foods and combinations of foods which can support human life is endless. While sharing the need to ingest the essential amino acids, fatty acids, vitamins, and minerals, human populations around the world have developed many ways of obtaining these essentials. The characteristics of dietary generalism have made it possible for human populations to exploit resources available in habitats far removed from the tropical forest homes of their primate ancestors. This capacity, among others, has made it possible for *Homo sapiens* to penetrate and colonize areas which would not seem fit for human habitation.

The distribution of human populations over the range of terrestrial habitats has placed them in a variety of ecological settings, each exerting somewhat different combinations of selective pressures. Many areas have been inhabited by a succession of prehominid and hominid populations spanning millions of years. Other areas have been more recently populated. But there is a sufficiently lengthy period of separation between various human populations to make the fact of their continued interfertility noteworthy. The ease of movement from one part of the world to another we enjoy today is a recent development. For the majority of human history, separation by distance was *de facto* reproductive isolation as well. Yet, when members of the most remote human groups meet and mate, as they show considerable enthusiasm for doing, the matings prove fertile and the offspring viable and fertile as well. Despite the variation which exists among the people of the world, there is no indication of incipient speciation anywhere. This is really a rather remarkable situation. It raises questions that are not only of significance to the understanding of our own species, but may have broad biological implications. Here again we encounter the consequences of a strategy of adaptability as opposed to one of adaptation.

The Limits of Tolerance to Nutritional Stress

One of the more vexing problems confronting nutritionists in the field is the assessment of nutritional status (Stini, 1978). Although the more extreme cases of nutritional deprivation can usually be diagnosed unambiguously, the majority of individuals at risk present a confusing picture of physiological and anthropometric variation. Two factors complicate the process of assessment. These are: 1) the wide range of adjustments invoked by the organism to permit survival in the face of nutritional stress, and 2) the degree of individual variability in invoking these adjustments. Preclinical cases of nutritional deprivation can be identified by using methods designed to reveal changes in biochemical characteristics signalling depletion of nutrient reserves. Thus, a severe reduction in serum proteins, including albumin and circulating antibodies, is indicative of depletion (Jelliffe, 1966). Also indicative is a lowering of the concentration of essential amino acids present in the serum, but it is seldom possible to make a reliable diagnosis on the basis of a single factor. This is so because in the otherwise-healthy individual, the defense mechanisms which come into play often mask the condition until the situation has reached a state of crisis. The demands of growth in younger individuals render them more unstable than adults. Thus, diagnosis of nutritional deprivation in infants and young children is at the same time more difficult and more crucial than for adults.

Starvation in Adults

Humans can survive extended fasts with surprisingly little damage. Young and Scrimshaw (1971) cite the example of Terence Mac Survey, an Irish revolutionist, who fasted for 74 days before dying of starvation in 1920. There are documented cases of obese humans living eight months without food and without ill effects. The length of survival is certainly related to the nutrient reserve of the individual. But that observation should not be interpreted as proof that weight loss during starvation is merely a matter of "living off one's fat." The manner in which the human body accommodates to prolonged food deprivation is more subtle and more complex than such a simple mechanism would encompass. Reference to the nutritional requirements of the human adult will give some reasons why this is so.

Energy requirements expressed as kilocalories per day increase with increasing body size. For instance, the basal calorie requirement of a 60 kilogram man is approximately 1630 kilocalories/day, while that of an 80 kilogram man is about 1933 kilocalories/day. Activity of increasing intensity will raise those requirements substantially. Table 11.1 gives some idea of the increase in calorie requirements associated with various levels of activity, and shows that both body size and activity levels combine to determine the total metabolic demand of an individual.

Table 11.1

Kilocalories per kilogram of body weight
per hour required for activity in humans

Activity	Men	Women
Very Light	1.5	1.3
Light	2.9	2.6
Moderate	4.3	4.1
Heavy	8.4	8.0

From: *Recommended Dietary Allowances* 8th ed. Washington, D.C., National Academy of Sciences, 1974.

Metabolic demand is also influenced by body composition. For instance, the basal requirements of a 70 kilogram man who is very lean are greater than those of a 70 kilogram man who is obese. Muscle is more active metabolically than fat tissue. This means that the obese individual not only carries a greater nutrient reserve, but, at similar activity levels, dissipates that reserve more slowly. For a species with a history of feast-and-famine cycles, this attribute has considerable potential value.

Protein requirements also increase with increasing body size. Again, the lean body mass is more significant than total body weight in the determination of protein requirements. The "biological value" of a protein is a function of its content of essential amino acids. These are isoleucine,

leucine, lysine, methionine, phenylalanine, threonine, tryptophan, and valine in the adult; all these plus histidene (and, possibly asparagene) in the growing individual. Wound healing, tissue replacement, and other processes relying upon protein synthesis all depend upon a steady supply of these essential amino acids.

The body maintains a dynamic equilibrium with respect to its amino acid constituents. The daily turnover of protein is generally greater than the dietary intake. The breakdown of proteins in tissue releases amino acids, some of which become constituents of newly synthesized proteins. But there is inevitably some loss of nitrogen released following the breakdown of amino acids. Some of this is excreted in the urine in the form of uric acid, urea, or creatinine. Other losses of nitrogen through excretion, sloughing, and secretion also occur. As a result, the need to maintain nitrogen balance determines the minimal level of protein intake the individual can tolerate. The protein requirements of humans thus represent two components: 1) specific amino acids, and 2) amino nitrogen. Table 11.2 lists the amino acid requirements of humans.

In addition to calorie and protein requirements, there is also the necessity of supplying the essential fatty acids. Linoleic and arachidonic acids are the only ones considered essential in humans. If sufficient linoleic acid is present,

Table 11.2

Estimated Amino Acid Requirements for Humans

Amino Acid	Infant (3-6 mo)	Child (10-12 yr)	Adult
Histidine	33	?	?
Isoleucine	80	28	12
Leucine	128	42	16
Lysine	97	44	12
Total S-containing amino acids	45	22	10
Total aromatic amino acids	132	22	16
Threonine	63	28	8
Tryptophan	19	4	3
Valine	89	25	14

Requirement (per kg of body wt.), mg/day

From: *Recommended Dietary Allowances* 8th ed. Washington, D.C., National Academy of Sciences, 1974.

arachidonic acid may be formed from it. But linoleic acid must always be ingested along with the fat and water soluble vitamins, a number of minerals, and, of course, water.

Confronted with all of these requirements, how is it possible for a human to sustain extended periods of starvation? Here is where certain aspects of our evolutionary history appear to have endowed us with some impressive defense mechanisms. In order to appreciate this endowment it is necessary to consider just how the human body responds to starvation.

Fasting leads to weight loss which does not follow a strictly linear course. This can be seen from the graph in figure 11.1. In the early stages of a fast, calorie demands are met by freeing up the glucose stored as glycogen in the liver. But this reserve is only sufficient for a few hours. A more important endogenous calorie source is the breakdown of amino acids released from tissue, primarily from skeletal muscle. The protein loss arising from reliance on this calorie resource is accompanied by the loss of a number of minerals. The resultant alterations in electrolyte balance cause a reduction in the water content of the body arising from physiological mechanisms concerned with maintenance of fluid homeostasis. This shedding of body water is the primary cause of the steep decline of weight characterizing the first five days of fast shown in figure 11.1.

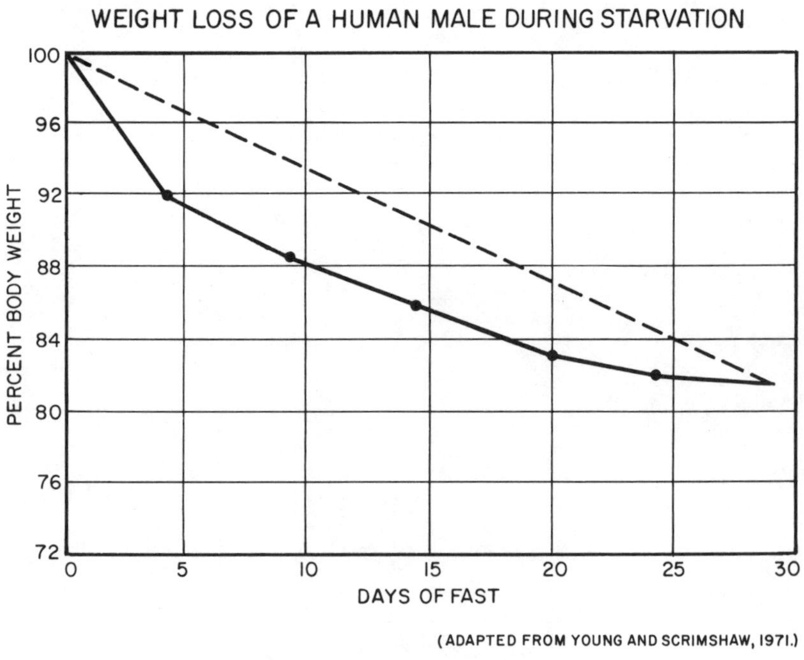

WEIGHT LOSS OF A HUMAN MALE DURING STARVATION

(ADAPTED FROM YOUNG AND SCRIMSHAW, 1971.)

Fig. 11.1

Subsequent weight loss increasingly involves the consumption of body fat. Since fat yields about nine kilocalories per gram, it constitutes a rich resource for the support of vital metabolic processes. In humans, the most crucial requirement is the support of a very demanding brain. In fact, in the resting state, the human brain consumes about two-thirds of the circulating glucose and about 45 percent of the oxygen supply. This means that the human brain requires, on the average, from 100 to 145 grams of glucose per day. That translates into 400 to 600 kilocalories, or from a quarter to a third of the body's total basal requirement.

At nine kilocalories per gram of fat consumed, just the basal requirements of a 70 kilogram man would require the consumption of about 200 grams of body fat (1800 kilocalories/day). Since it is unlikely that activity would be so reduced that the metabolic rate would not rise above the basal level, the actual requirements of the starving man will exceed the basal rate. Figure 11.1 shows that from days four to nine, a 63 kilogram male lost about four percent of his original body weight over a five day period. This amounts to roughly 500 grams/day, much of it presumably representing fat consumption. This rate of loss slows with the passage of time, until it attains a value of about 100 grams/day after the twenty-fifth day of fast. In an obese individual, nearly all calorie requirements can be supplied by such fat consumption for an extended period.

When calorie requirements are supplied by consumption of body fat, it appears that the number of cells in fatty tissue remains essentially unaltered while the individual cells give up their fat content. In a study of obese adults fed just 600 kilocalories/day, Hersch found that, while losing as much as 100 pounds, his subjects showed a shrinkage of about 45 percent in the size of adipose cells. This gives some idea of the impressive energy storage capacity an obese human adult possesses (cited in Young and Scrimshaw, 1971).

But the maintenance of all human metabolic needs cannot be sustained through metabolic consumption of the triglycerides freed from human fat. This is because, although amino acids can be consumed as a calorie resource, sugars and fats cannot replace the amino acids and nitrogen essential to maintain tissue proteins. Thus, reliance upon a diet deficient in protein, more specifically one deficient in essential amino acids, will lead to a negative nitrogen balance and, eventually, some loss of tissue. Severe and prolonged imbalance or deficit in amino acid intake will result in actual loss of skeletal muscle fibers (Stini, 1975b). Destruction of muscle cells, including some cardiac muscle, can assume significant proportions even while fat stores persist. For instance, in one clinically-documented case, a 20-year-old girl weighing 260 pounds fasted for 30 weeks, reducing her weight to 132 pounds. She developed a severe cardiac arrhythmia shortly after ending her fast. Despite prompt medical intervention, she died of ventricular fibrillation. Her autopsy revealed that she had consumed half of her body's lean tissue mass. Most significantly, she had consumed part of the fibrous tissue of her heart muscle (Garnett, cited in Young and Scrimshaw, 1971).

Muscle tissue exchanges amino acids with tissue fluids on a regular basis. Thus, muscle is far from being the static structural protein it is sometimes thought. The exchange of amino acids is usually a balanced one, however, with muscle fibers gaining as much as they lose in the normal course of events. But in times of serious deprivation, whether it be a calorie or amino acid lack, the amino acids given up by muscle may not be replaced. They may instead be directed to other, higher priority functions, such as synthesis of antibodies or protection of liver function, or they may be metabolized as a calorie resource. In some cases, both forms of allocation may occur simultaneously. When amino acid loss reaches sufficiently high levels, muscle fibers may be lost. But this is not usually the case. Improvement of nutritional intake will result in the replenishment of muscle amino acid complement and, if circumstances warrant, allow withdrawal again in future times of need.

Other sources of amino acids available to the starving human include the breakdown of digestive enzymes in the small intestine (Stini, 1971), and the catabolism of serum proteins, most notably albumin. But these are very limited sources which only serve as a temporary cushion against sudden depletion. They do, along with certain behavioral alterations, facilitate the transition to reliance upon endogenous reserves while maintaining physiological homeostasis to a surprisingly high degree.

When starvation is of sufficient duration to produce significant changes in body composition, activity levels are drastically reduced. This profound lethargy produces an important reduction in the metabolic demand for nutrients. When activity is reduced in this manner, interest in sex is totally absent. Victims of starvation consistently relate that lack of contact with persons of the opposite sex was a matter of no concern to them, even though such deprivation in some cases lasted for several years. Clearly, sexual activity under such circumstances would be maladaptive in its consequences. Its discontinuation, along with that of other forms of activity, may well spell the difference between survival and death.

From the foregoing, it should be evident that a healthy adult can draw upon considerable endogenous resources to survive a period of starvation. Prioritizing the functions to which scarce resources are channeled will usually serve to maintain the immune response even though the synthesis of antibodies requires the depletion of amino acid reserves. There is considerable variation in the degree to which such channeling favors maintenance of immune competence, but the mechanisms underlying it appear to be a universal biological trait. Thus, while starved adults do become more susceptible to a variety of infectious diseases, there are many remarkable examples of survival in the presence of some of the most virulent pathogens.

The Special Problems of the Growing Individual

The threat to survival posed by starvation is much greater for the growing child than for the adult. There are a number of reasons for the difference. First, the demands of growth draw heavily upon the supply of a variety of nutrients. Growth means protein synthesis, which translates into high demand for essential amino acids. In the young, growing individual, endogenous reserves are seldom sufficient to sustain both growth and maintenance for any appreciable length of time. Moreover, the very young child, confronted for the first time by a variety of infectious diseases, experiences recurrent demands upon the immune system. It is not surprising, therefore, that severe consequences can arise from an encounter with otherwise mild and self-limited diseases such as measles, chicken pox, or pertussis. The appearance of the symptoms of kwashiorkor following a case of measles often betrays the fact that the child was barely able to sustain all the demands for amino acids before the added burden of infection and heightened immunoglobulin synthesis. Under such conditions, immunization is dangerous (Katz, 1977).

The statistics on infant and child mortality and morbidity in areas of chronic nutritional inadequacy are evidence of the vulnerability of the growing child to a variety of conditions. In view of the severity of the stress and the fundamental processes which are threatened, what is perhaps most remarkable is the large number of individuals who manage somehow to survive. Here human adaptability can be seen to produce phenotypic alterations great enough to resemble genetic changes. Many population differences in body size, long thought to be evidence of genetic variation between human groups, have been found to be largely the product of alterations in the growth process induced by nutritional stress. Such changes belong to the broad category of "developmental acclimatizations" (Stini, 1975). They are the end product of a combination of physiological adjustments which serve to reduce the rate of growth while maintaining allometric relationships between body proportions.

The effective reduction in body size attainable by allometric decreases in growth are only now being recognized for what they really represent. With substantial increases in body size occurring in many parts of the world, it has become increasingly clear that the environment has played a major role in the determination of adult morphology. The changes currently occurring are taking place much too swiftly — sometimes within a single generation — to be explained as the product of genetic change. Thus, the "secular trend" toward increasing body size around the world serves as retrospective evidence of human adaptation to factors, including nutritional ones, which put limits on the growth process (Tanner, 1968). We have indications that the human phenotype has the capacity to attain dimensions suited to the limitations of the habitat. This capacity, *optimization* of growth, contrasts with what is frequently viewed as the hallmark of good health — *maximization* of growth. The biological payoff is substantial.

Table 11.3 compares the calorie and protein requirements of a 70 kilogram and a 60 kilogram man. As the comparison shows, the smaller man requires considerably less from his environment than does the larger. In most cases, proportional reductions in size cause little if any reduction in functional capacity to do work. This is especially so when the work performed is at the submaximal level. Most sustained human activities are of a sort that permits a smaller individual to perform as well or better than a larger one. So, in many cases, reductions in body size permit larger numbers of individuals to survive on a given resource base. The biological implications are clear: the survival of human populations in a world of uncertain food supply may well depend upon some means of maintaining population numbers at the expense of individual body growth. In essence, the strategy of adaptability is to divide the supportable biomass among the largest number of individuals, which insures survival for the population while at the same time facilitating individual survival by reducing demand.

Table 11.3

Comparison of Calorie Requirements of a 70 kg U.S. male
with those of a 60 kg Colombian male at similar activity levels

	U.S.A.	Colombia
Mean Body Weight (kg)	70	60
Calorie Costs (kcal)		
Resting (8 hrs.)	570	480
Very Light Activity (6 hrs.)	630	540
Light Labor (8 hrs.)	1624	1392
Moderate Labor (2 hrs.)	602	516
TOTAL	3462	2928

Human Sexual Dimorphism:
Anatomical Indicators of Functional Differences

While size reductions in males are adaptive within limits defined by work capacity, there are special constraints with respect to females. Reproductive success depends upon the ability to carry a fetus to term and to support the newborn infant through lactation. Both gestation and lactation require additional calories and protein. But there is no guarantee that the additional requirements can be satisfied at the time they occur. It is therefore essential that the human female be able to maintain endogenous reserves of both calories and amino acids to permit successful reproduction even when supplementary nutrition is unavailable. Skeletal muscle, the primary site of amino acid reserves, is a crucial element in the maintenance of these reserves. If females were to reduce lean body mass to the same relative extent that males do, their ability to bear and nurture offspring would be threatened. So the strategy of human adaptability dictates that in populations of recurrent nutritional inadequacy, sexual dimorphism for lean body mass will be less than in well fed populations. Table 11.4 shows a comparison of the upper-arm muscle circumference of males and females of a well-fed population (U.S.) and one in which nutritional intake had been very marginal (Heliconia, Colombia). Comparison of these figures gives an indication of the degree to which sexual differences in skeletal muscle volume can be altered even while both sexes continue to function with a traditional division of labor.

Table 11.4

Mean upper arm muscle circumference of adults of
both sexes from a U.S. and a Colombian population

	Colombia		U.S.A.		Colombia % of U.S.A.	
	Area (mm^2)	Weight (kg)	Area (mm^2)	Weight (kg)	Area (mm^2)	Weight (kg)
Male	4267	60	6464	70	66	85
Female	3450	51	4272	58	81	88
Female % of Male	81	85	66	83		

From an evolutionary perspective, one crucial element stands out in determining the functional and anatomical differences between the sexes. That is, women bear and nurture children. Thus, whatever the status of sexual division of labor, there is one form of labor that cannot be shared. This may seem a trivially obvious fact, but so many other factors derive from it that it warrants careful attention.

Fundamentally, males are male because their role in the reproductive process is to inseminate females, while the characteristics of females are the product of adaptations which permit the fertilization of the eggs she carries. Up to this point, the relationship between the sexes is essentially a symmetrical one. But this symmetry quickly breaks down once fertilization has been accomplished. The burden of childbearing falls most heavily on the mother. Regardless of the social system to which the father belongs, his adjustments are largely psychological and behavioral. Those of the mother involve widespread physiological changes. The investment in the newborn's survival is much greater for the mother than for the father. While it has received half of its genetic instructions from each parent, virtually all of the substances needed to permit those instructions to be carried out come to the developing fetus via its mother. Many, perhaps most, of the proteins making up the tissues and organs of the newborn are synthesized from amino acids which were once part of the tissues and organs of its mother.

Certainly the intimacy of this relationship between mother and fetus is a highly evolved, highly adaptive characteristic. The extension of this close relationship well beyond the event of birth is equally adaptive for the species. This is so because a human baby is essentially an extero-uterine fetus for the first six to nine months following birth. As such, it is totally dependent upon its mother for its nutritional requirements. This prolonged intimate relationship is not without risks. Any event that separates mother and infant for a prolonged period threatens the life of the infant. Undoubtedly, in the history of the human species, the difficulty of sustaining a fetus through gestation and an infant through a lengthy period of dependency led to many infant deaths. If there were not strong selective advantages inherent in the system which offset the cost such deaths represent, persistent selective pressure would have favored the shortening of this period of dependency. The species would then pursue the more common strategy of producing larger numbers of offspring among whom mortalities would be high. One of the outstanding characteristics of human adaptation is the degree to which we, as a species, have opted for a low reproductive rate coupled with a complex of mechanisms which maximize infant survival.

A successful means of maintaining population size and variability is essential to evolutionary success. This may seem another trivially obvious statement, but the means by which success is attained differ from species to species. The human solution to the problem of balancing maintenance of population size against the maintenance of variability has favored the latter. This is true despite the impressive increase in the world's human population in recent times. The paradox of rapid population increase in a species which evolved favoring "quality" over "quantity" is resolved when it is seen that factors which strongly influenced human evolution have quite recently been modified through cultural mechanisms. Nonetheless, we as a species bear the physiological and anatomical evidence of our evolutionary history, and the nature and degree of human sexual dimorphism is part of our heritage which recent events have done little to change.

Maternal Nutrition and Successful Reproduction

Many anatomical features of the human female reflect the requirements of the childbearing process. Some of the structures involved are those associated with fertilization, others with parturition, and others with sustenance. It is the last-mentioned which will be of primary concern here. This is because the features which are associated with fertilization, although anatomically definitive, do not represent an assymetrical commitment with respect to the sexes. The anatomical structures associated with parturition, while revealing both definitive and assymetrical differences, are capable of few alterations which are compatible with successful reproduction. Thus, environmental factors which might alter the degree of sexual dimorphism in a population are less easily detected through anatomical features associated with fertilization and parturition than is the case with those associated with sustenance.

The crucial nature of female adaptation to nutritional inadequacies is self evident. Adjustments in the rate of growth and maturation are central to that adaptation. Thus, while males undergo similar stresses, there is a high probability that their response will differ; this is because the energy investment of the male is both qualitatively and quantitatively different than that of the female.

An important aspect of the female adjustment is the retention of a reserve of amino acids and calories maintained in the muscle and fat compartments. The amount of energy stored by the time of menarche has been calculated at 75,000 to 90,000 kilocalories (Frisch, 1972). This reserve would, under most circumstances, be adequate to support a full gestation period and to initiate lactation. However, the total calorie cost of pregnancy may, under some circumstances, exceed the reserve (Blackburn and Calloway, 1976a, 1976b). Recurrent pregnancies under conditions of nutritional inadequacy may act to deplete maternal reserves substantially. The effect of such depletion may be most pronounced during the postnatal period. Lactation, beginning during this time of depletion, may create demands on maternal resources which cannot be satisfied.

Lactation after depletion of maternal reserves might be expected to affect the volume and/or the composition of milk produced. Most evidence available in the 1970's supported the position that it is volume rather than composition which is adjusted. But studies of variations in the composition of human milk, both between and within individual mothers, have cast some doubt on the universality of volumetric rather than compositional adjustment.

Whether maternal adjustments favor changes in volume or composition of milk in the first or subsequent trimesters post-partum, the state of depletion of the mother will be an important determinant of the change. The factors which provide a measure of the capacity of the mother to sustain pregnancy and lactation are measureable in part through analysis of maternal body composition. Here it is necessary to take into account the status of both fat depots and lean body mass. It is perhaps the latter which is most significant, since amino acids drawn from skeletal muscle serve as endogenous reserves for protein synthesis and for gluconeogenesis. Alanine is the primary endogenous glucogenic substrate released by muscle and extracted by the liver during starvation and, quantitatively, alanine concentrations are among the highest in plasma. Thus, a fall in plasma alanine may impair hepatic gluconeogenesis and lead to maternal hypoglycemia.

In well-fed populations, women add between one and one and one half kilograms of lean tissue during the last half of pregnancy. This is approximately equal to the amount of fat gain during the same interval. In general, adequately nourished pregnant women take up nitrogen at about 25-30 percent efficiency, there being a linear relationship between calorie intake and nitrogen balance.

The real stress for the inadequately nourished woman comes with the onset of lactation. Supplementation begun in the post partum period may well be too late to compensate for the increased need for both protein and calories experienced at this time. As has been argued by Habicht et al. (1974), the maximum benefit from supplementation would accrue from beginning early in pregnancy. Failing in this, supplementation of the mother still has distinct advantages, both from the standpoint of maternal and infant health, and in terms of economy (McKigney, 1971; Jelliffe and Jelliffe, 1976; Sosa et al., 1976).

Concluding Remarks

The evolutionary history of our species has been such that humans are nutritional generalists. The ability to survive using a range of nutrient resources has permitted human colonization of a wide range of habitats outside the original tropical one. By expansion, colonization, and exploitation of a variety of habitats, our species has become increasingly committed to a strategy featuring maximization of individual survival. Physiological mechanisms which permit phenotypic alterations within the lifetime of the individual are a central element of this strategy.

A second significant point is that even for a species which emphasizes individual survival, successful reproduction remains a fundamental considera-tion. In a world full of uncertainties, where environmental changes of great magnitude have occurred throughout the history of the species, mechanisms which safeguard the capacity to bear and rear offspring take on special significance. Human gestation is a lengthy 280 days. The relative period of post partum dependency is extraordinarily long, even in comparison to that of other mammals. Thus, there is strong likelihood that, during the period of one and one-half to two years it takes to bring a human infant from conception through lactation, at least some period of nutritional stress will occur. In order for the human mother to buffer her offspring from the threat such stresses pose, it is essential that she be able to accumulate and draw upon endogenous stores of essential nutrients. Consequently, there are special limitations imposed upon the phenotypic adjustments made by females as compared to males who grow and develop under similar conditions of nutritional inadequacy.

Males are larger and have greater lean body mass than females. This has been thought to be associated with the necessities created by differential demands for strenuous physical activity arising from longstanding practices involving division of labor between the sexes. Since there is greater flexibility in the activity pattern than in requirements for reproductive success, males tend to be more developmentally labile than females. The net result is a reduction in sexual dimorphism for muscle mass under conditions of nutritional inadequacy. From the standpoint of population energetics, this gives evidence of being a strategy of considerable merit. Both individual and population survival — seemingly conflicting goals — are thus promoted by the mechanisms cited.

References

Blackburn, M.W., and D.H. Calloway
1976a Basal metabolic rate and energy expenditures of mature, pregnant women. *Journal of the American Dietetic Association 69:* 24.

Blackburn, M.W., and D.H. Calloway
1976b Energy expenditure and consumption of mature, pregnant and lactating women. *Journal of the American Dietetic Association 69:* 29.

Frisch, R.
1972 Weight at menarche: similarity for well-nourished and undernourished girls at differing ages and evidence for historical constancy. *Pediatrics 50:* 445.

Habicht, J.P., C. Yarbrough, A. Lechting, and R.E. Klein
1974 Relation of maternal supplementary feeding during pregnancy to birth weight and other sociobiological factors. In *Nutrition and Fetal Development,* M. Winick, ed., John Wiley and Sons, New York, p. 127.

Jelliffe, D.B.
1966 The Assessment of the Nutritional Status of the Community. World Health Organization, Geneva.

Jelliffe, D.B., and E.F.P. Jelliffe
1976 Letter—The cost of breast feeding. *Lancet* 21 February, 1976, p. 420.

Katz, Michael
1977 Immunization in malnourished children—a review. In *Malnutrition and the Immune Response,* R.M. Suskind, ed., Raven Press, New York, p. 421.

McKigney, J.
1971 Economic aspects. *American Journal of Clinical Nutrition, 24:* 1005.

Sinclair, H.M.
1953 The diet of Canadian Indians and Eskimos. Nutrition Society, *Proceedings,* Vol. 12, Cambridge University Press, London.

Slobodkin, L.B.
1968 Toward a predictive theory of evolution. In *Population Biology and Evolution,* R.C. Lewontin, ed., Syracuse University Press, Syracuse.

Sosa, R., M. Klaus, and J.J. Urrutia
1976 Feed the nursing mother, thereby the infant. *Journal of Pediatrics 88:* 668.

Stini, W.A.
1971   Evolutionary implications of changing nutritional patterns in human
                populations. *American Anthropologist 73:*1019.

Stini, W.A.
1975a   *Ecology and Human Adaptation.* W.C. Brown, Dubuque, Iowa.

Stini, W.A.
1975b   Adaptive Strategies of human populations under nutritional stress. In
                Biosocial Interrelations in Population Adaptation, E. Watts, F.E.
                Johnston, and G.W. Lasker, eds., Mouton Publishers, The Hague.

Stini, W.A.
1978   ✓ The concept and assessment of nutritional status. In *Anthropological
                Aspects of Human Nutrition,* F.E. Johnston, ed., School of American
                Research, Santa Fe, New Mexico.

Tanner, J.M.
1968   Earlier maturation in man. *Scientific American 218:*21.

Wilson, E.O., and W.H. Bossert
1971   *A Primer of Population Biology.* Sinauer Associates, Stamford, Conn.

Young, V.R., and N.S. Scrimshaw
1971   The physiology of starvation. *Scientific American 225:*14.

Strategies For Solving World Food Problems

Gail Grigsby Harrison

The basic facts of malnutrition in the world have been known for some years. Between 400 and 500 million people suffer from protein-calorie malnutrition, and additional millions from other forms of malnutrition (Austin, 1975). Population is growing at an exponential rate, while worldwide food production has barely kept pace on a per capita basis, in spite of advances in agricultural productivity. The immediate cause of most malnutrition, however, is not lack of aggregate food supplies, but maldistribution − unequal access to food. Total world grain production was about 1.3 billion metric tons in the late 1970's. If evenly distributed, this grain would provide annually about 3000 kilocalories of energy and 65 grams of protein per day for each of the four billion people on earth, without considering contributions from pulses, fruits, and vegetables, fish, or animal products (Timmer, n.d.). Disparity between diets in the developed and the developing countries, and maldistribution of food within the developing countries, and even within households, seem to assure that the poorest and most vulnerable to malnutrition are those with the least power to influence policy or to exert economic influence on the market-place.

Nutritional deficiencies in developing countries are principally and directly the result of widespread poverty. It is tempting to assume, therefore, that, with general socioeconomic development, the problems of malnutrition will disappear. This point of view was prevalent in the 1950's and 1960's, and was consistent with a one-sided view of development, which assumed that diffusion of technology from the developed to the developing nations would alleviate the worst of poverty's manifestations. Slowness in successfully adopting this technology was attributed to the cultural conservatism of agrarian societies (Marchione, 1977). As Adams has stated, the general concern of those involved with development was to make more of it (Adams, 1974).

Since 1970, several facts have become clear which bring this point of view into question. First, rising national incomes, especially in developing countries, do not always guarantee better diets. Rising gross national product may first appear as profit in the pockets of the economically advantaged in the developing countries, without bettering the lot of the poorest consumers.

Further, demands other than food costs are made upon individual incomes, and rising incomes are usually accompanied by increased exposure to non-food consumer goods. Second, malnutrition itself impairs the progress of development through its effect on the ability of workers to produce and the ability of children and adults to take advantage of educational opportunities (Berg, 1973).

Thus, the point of view of development planners has changed, to the extent that a working document from the 1974 World Food Conference stated: ". . . it is neither necessary nor desirable to wait until the process of economic development has brought about a general increase in incomes. Action . . . can be taken in the short term to increase the food production capacity, the purchasing power, and/or the nutritional status of the least advantaged people in each country" (World Food Conference, 1974). The goal of singling out the reduction of malnutrition as a specific objective of development policy has become widely accepted, albeit for different reasons in different circles. Some argue that reduction in deprivation is a legitimate indicator rather than a by-product of development, while others feel that the reduction of malnutrition will have a positive effect on the gross national product (Reutlinger, 1976).

Recognizing the legitimacy of this goal, however, is only the first step. Formulating and implementing policy which will reduce malnutrition is much more complicated. The decision to deploy resources to alleviate malnutrtion is a political one, which takes place in an economic and social context; further, the nature of nutritional problems poses difficulties seldom encountered in other spheres of development.

The World Food and Nutrition Study

During 1976, the writer was a member of the Nutrition Overview Study Team of the World Food and Nutrition Study undertaken by the National Research Council, National Academy of Sciences. President Ford directed the Academy to undertake the study, following Secretary of State Kissinger's statement at the World Food Conference, in 1974, committing the United States to a leadership role in alleviating hunger and malnutrition. The summary report of the study was delivered to President Carter in June, 1977; it was based upon the individual reports of fourteen study teams, and was compiled by a steering committee. Full reports by the individual study teams were published as a four-volume supplement to the summary report (National Academy of Sciences, 1977). Of the fourteen study teams appointed, only one was concerned specifically with nutrition. This study team was chaired by Alan Berg, of the World Bank, with Doris Calloway as co-chairman. Its task was to define the priorities for research which would have a maximum impact on hunger and malnutrition.

The study team began by calling upon the expertise of a broad base of nutrition scientists and program personnel from the U.S. and abroad. Study team members formed satellite groups (48 individuals in all) to assist in sorting through the many research possibilities posed to the team. In addition, 140 specialists, representing a wide range of disciplines and countries, reviewed the team's working papers at various stages. Opinions were exchanged with 58 of these specialists at hearings in Boston, New York, Washington, and Berkeley. Those from the international nutrition community sent written or taped responses.

The study team based its work on the following assumptions: a) that realistic and equitable national and international food and nutrition policies must be formulated; b) that the prevalence of malnutrition in many countries has been and will continue to be related to government decisions on economic development strategies and other non-health concerns; and c) that political leaders in many countries have responded to the pressure to provide food to people who need it. The magnitude of expenditures is such that accelerated research is almost an imperative to assure more rational, efficient use of increasingly scarce food and financial resources.

Research priorities were selected on the basis of the following criteria: a) Does this research problem address a gap in knowledge which directly impedes progress in policy decision-making? b) Can it be accomplished? c) Has it been receiving insufficient attention? Only research topics which met all three criteria were included in the final report.

A further assumption which underlies the report, and which colored the deliberations of the study team, was the realization that a "we/they" distinction between the developed and developing nations is not only politically inappropriate, but would be counterproductive in terms of U.S. priorities. We deal with the same nutritional unknowns as do the developing countries. Research conducted in the developing countries will have increasing applicability in the U.S. and vice versa.

The completed report was quite different from research recommendations usually seen in agriculture or basic science. While increased funding for basic nutrition research was encouraged, emphasis was given to areas which impede policy decisions. The term "political will" found its way into the final study report in a prominent place, stating clearly that both intensified research *and* political will are necessary if problems are to be solved. The Steering Committee's summary document stated that food production in the developing countries will have to be doubled by the end of the century. Little of the increase is expected to come from additional land put under cultivation; rather, it will come from increased yields — especially through agricultural methods which make minimal energy demands — and through better food preservation and decreased food losses. As stated in a report published in *Science,* the study ". . . is a creature of the 1970's. It pulls away from the moon shot mentality of the Green Revolution, recognizing instead that obstacles raised by politics, population, and poverty have to be overcome if increased production is to make a dent on the food problem" (Holden, 1977).

While the importance of production is recognized, especially in the long run, there is also a need to focus on consumption, on demand rather than supply, and on consumers rather than, and in relation to, producers. As often as not, malnutrition is caused by an unequal distribution of food supplies rather than by inadequate aggregate supplies (Reutlinger, 1976).

With this focus, the study team delineated four major areas of research which were recommended for priority funding:

a) the functional significance of nutritional status;
b) ensuring the quality, safety, and adequacy of diets as consumed;
c) intervening to improve the nutritional status of selected groups;
d) nutritional impact of government policies.

Each of these areas has specific significance for nutrition policy development.

Nutrition Policy Defined

Food and nutrition policy may be defined as ". . . a complex of educational, economic, technical, and legislative measures designed to reconcile, at a level judged feasible by the planner, projected food demand, forecast food supply, and nutritional requirements . . . (the policy is) directed at remedying distortions detrimental to the public interest between what the consumer desires, what he can obtain, and what he needs physiologically" (World Food Conference, 1974).

Nutritional planning implies several things. First, nutrition objectives must be seen in the context of other valid national objectives. Resources directed toward the alleviation of malnutrition must be measured against potential benefit, and the cost/benefit ratio compared with that projected from alternate investment of the resources. Second, the planner requires three types of information: accurate projection of food supply, accurate estimate of food demand, and knowledge of nutritional requirements. Lack of adequate information in any of these sectors will impede efficient decision-making. Third, a food and nutrition policy will consist of a number of policies and programs (what Austin has called a "portfolio" of measures) suited to the local conditions and resources, and responsive to the particular etiology of malnutrition in the local situation (Austin 1975).

Functional Significance of Nutritional Status

The severity and extent of a country's food deficit is usually described in terms of the disparity between food supply and requirements. These data, even if broken down by geographic region, do not provide necessary information on who is malnourished and to what extent. Concern is with the degree to which a given food intake maintains, enhances, or inhibits an individual's functional performance (activity, growth, resistance to infection, and so forth), rather than with the food consumption of an entire population group. But even careful surveys of nutritional status, based on physical and biochemical findings, as well as dietary information, do not provide data on the consequences or costs of malnutrition. A simple boundary does not exist for any nutrient between adequate and inadequate intakes. Rather, levels of food required, amounts consumed, and levels of performance are closely interrelated.

To decide which nutrition problems should receive priority, and how resources should be allocated among target groups, the decision-maker needs to know the relative seriousness of different degrees of malnutrition and the amount of benefit to be derived from specific increments of nutritional improvement. The percentage of the world population with mild to moderate malnutrition far exceeds the proportion with severe malnutrition. Is it more important to use food resources to bring the majority who are mildly malnourished up to optimal levels (if these can be defined), or is it more important to eradicate *severe* malnutrition? It is usually assumed that returns from improvements decrease as nutritional state improves, but this is not necessarily true for all functions and at all levels of intake. There may be thresholds below which increments have no demonstrable benefit.

The question of standards for nutritional adequacy is central to the issue of functional significance. Dietary standards are determined on varying amounts of data, usually obtained on subjects in highly artificial conditions. The real world fact is that people live in multi-stress environments and are often adapted, genetically or physiologically (or both), to those environments in various ways (Haas and Harrison, 1977). Nutrient requirements may be quite different in a cold versus a hot climate, in a high-altitude versus a sea-level environment, under conditions of heavy physical work versus sedentary work. The original studies of human protein requirements were conducted under conditions of calorie adequacy; only recently have investigators begun to look experimentally at protein requirements under conditions of a marginal, inadequate, or excessive calorie supply. Ideal rates of human growth have not been defined; the idea that bigger is necessarily better is being seriously questioned, but there are many unresolved issues. At what stages of development are growth rates critical? Is there an optimum body size? At what stage or degree are changes irreversible for a given function? Politically, is reversibility an academic question when prevention is cheaper than cure? How much variability is there in individual capacity to adapt to altered nutritional states?

It is clear that rapid, simple measurements of nutritional status are required; measurements of functional performance must be developed and quantified. The determination of calorie and protein needs should receive priority. In contrast, the cost of providing micronutrients is nominal. The major cost of providing these micro-nutrients is in delivery, and corrective measures do not require that individual dietary requirements be closely defined.

Ensuring the Quality, Safety, and Adequacy of Diets

Little is known about the long-term significance of the variety of human diets. Human populations subsist on diets in which as little as two percent or as much as 50 percent of the energy is derived from fat and eight percent to 20 percent from protein — with almost all or virtually none from animal sources — and in which the carbohydrate is mainly present as refined foods or as unrefined roots and cereals. Important interactions exist between nutritional and non-nutritional components of the diet. In many instances, adequate combinations of foods (such as maize and beans, or rice and fish) have developed indigenously, as has fortification of foods with plant ash or crude salt, fermentation, yeast, and lime. Rather than being replaced with technological alternatives, traditional food processes should be studied in an effort to improve on their nutritional contribution by increasing yield and assuring safety.

Along with a focus on traditional diets and food preparation processes, information is badly needed on the factors which influence household and individual eating behavior. Manifestations of poverty, such as poor housing, poor sanitation, and illiteracy can be largely remedied by delivering an extensive infrastructure of public services. Changes in nutritional status, however, depend on how individual households respond to the stimuli of public intervention. Households are the ultimate decision-making units concerning nutritional intake, and it is in this context that public policies have to be designed (Reutlinger, 1976). Locally relevant information is needed in each country on the significance of factors that determine consumer-level dietary behavior: income, prices, household size and composition, social and cultural determinants of food choices and food distribution within the family, local food production and distribution patterns, and relevant knowledge and attitudes. The effect of both planned and unplanned change on dietary patterns and nutritional status should be assessed. There is a need to know about variability in the efficiency with which family resources are used to provide nutrition.

This set of research questions, more than any other in the entire National Academy of Sciences study, addresses the concern that, whatever else, science should "do no harm." Change in food systems, planned or not, is inevitable. Both planned and unplanned changes are occurring in a vacuum of information. There is a critical need for inexpensive methods of monitoring short-run changes in food consumption patterns, and for culturally appropriate techniques for gathering valid information on food consumption by individuals within eating groups.

High priority should be given to research regarding nutrition in populations and subpopulations which are malnourished. However, long-range benefits may justify expenditures to learn about behavior that maintains adequate nutritional status in the face of environmental and social changes, and determinants of dietary behavior in affluent populations. Food consumption patterns in affluent populations affect the food available to the rest of the world, often set the pattern for widespread changes in food habits, and determine the nutritional status and functioning of the affluent populations themselves.

Intervening to Improve the
Nutritional Status of Selected Groups

Feeding programs have been and continue to be the most important way to give direct and immediate nutritional help to the most needy groups of people, be they refugees from a natural or human disaster, young children and pregnant women, or the poorest of poor families. Feeding programs, when carried out with appropriate foods for an adequate length of time, can ensure a minimum level of nutrition to those most vulnerable, who cannot meet their needs through the marketplace. In addition, successful feeding programs can help improve the health and educational services in developing countries by reducing hospitalization for malnutrition and absenteeism from schools. However, there have been many negative side effects of feeding programs. Probably most important, when the programs have been based on imported foods, they have often resulted in significant depression of local production of food because of a lowering of prices. This has been the case even with the provision of food in the wake of disaster (World Food Conference, 1974). Some feeding programs have brought about problems if they were suddenly and inappropriately discontinued, and others have failed because of lack of appropriate administrative infrastructure, planning, and organization.

A major problem with the history of feeding programs has been inadequate evaluation. We do not, in spite of decades of experience, have an adequate information base on which to build decisions. We can, to be sure, avoid the most obvious mistakes of the past — provision of culturally unacceptable foods, abrupt discontinuance of a program — but we do not have adequate information for a planner to decide, for example, whether it is better to direct supplementary feeding to children or to workers; whether it is better to combine a feeding program and a family planning program, or to leave them separate; whether it is better to provide, given scarce resources, two-thirds of the recommended daily allowance of calories to one-third of the needy children, or one-third of the needed calories to two-thirds of the needy children.

Many other direct interventions besides feeding programs are possible. These, too, need evaluation. Some of these are:

Multi-tiered pricing systems. Basic staples can be sold at less than market cost. An example is the system of fair price shops in India, which insure the quality and price of the food. An alternative approach is a direct subsidy to poor consumers (via food stamps or coupons) which enable purchase of all food or specific foods (such as weaning foods) at less than market price.

Direct rationing of basic commodities. Rationing reminds Americans of wartime, but it is a useful means of limiting the effect of high purchasing power on basic food prices, and hence on access to basic foods for the poor.

Nutrient supplementation and fortification. Many foods have been fortified with many nutrients, in many places. The only proven and dramatic successes have been in programs to add iodine to salt in goiterous regions and to add vitamin D to milk. Other additions − lysine to corn, B vitamins to bread, iron to various foods, vitamin A to sugar, and so on − need further testing. Sustained improvement has not been documented. To be effective, fortification must reach the subpopulation group most in need, must not make the fortified foods unacceptable, and must not pose risks to other, better nourished segments of the population.

The introduction of new foods. New foods have been introduced in many cultures in both planned and unplanned situations. Some new foods have been successes, others failures. We know too little about the reasons why.

Nutrition education. Nutrition education is the most widespread form of nutrition intervention. Success, in spite of isolated exceptions, has been minimal or undocumented. Unsupported by a sound framework of nutrition policies, education programs function as an arm without a body (World Food Conference, 1974). There is some evidence that education is effective when backed up by a coherent policy. We need, however, to know a great deal more about the factors that determine food-related behavior.

Nutritional Impact of Government Policies

Policies designed to have an impact on sanitation, housing, health, international trade, credit, inflation, employment, population control, migration, markets, transportation, and agriculture all have effects on nutrition. They are, however, seldom made with this impact in mind. To anticipate the effects on nutrition — to require a "nutritional impact statement" of any proposed government policy — would be to make nutrition truly a national priority. Some of the issues related to non-food government policies include:

Production strategies. What are the nutritional consequences of encouraging commercial vs. subsistence crops? Monoculture vs. integrated, diversified plots? Providing assistance to larger, more productive farmers vs. needier, small-scale farmers?

Agricultural research strategies. What are the nutritional benefits or detriments to be derived from research on one type of crop vs. another? On energy-intensive vs. labor-intensive methods of increasing production?

Rural credit programs. Which crops are eligible? On what inputs can credit be spent — why on tractors but not day laborers?

Food self-sufficiency. Some countries are specifying increasing food self-sufficiency as a national goal. Is "food independence" the best way to achieve nutritional well-being? What degree of independence? Should a country strive to be self-sufficient in bread but not flour? in flour but not wheat? in wheat but not combines? in combines but not in diesel fuel? To what degree is food independence desirable in an interdependent world?

Food aid. In what contexts do the long term effects on local production outweigh the short term benefits?

Resource use. Is there a conflict between dietary patterns of wealthy countries and poor ones? It costs several times more to feed a citizen of the U.S. than a citizen of India, in terms of dollars, grain, and non-renewable resources. The access/distribution issue exists within and between countries. Whether changes toward less ecologically expensive diets in the developed countries would have measurable benefits on the rest of the world (aside from the probable benefits to our own health) can be studied. This is an area in which good research could shed considerable light while dissipating some of the heat.

Nutrition Policy: The Jamaican Example

Food and nutrition policies are being formulated and implemented by some countries. As early as 1972, a newly-elected Jamaican government was emphasizing the theme "Grow Our Own Food," and by 1974 had formulated

three clear objectives (Marchione, 1977):
(1) Ensure availability of sufficient food by 1980 to maintain good nutrition and dietary well-being for all segments of the population.
(2) Ensure annual increases in the proportion of energy and protein requirements supplied by local production.
(3) Eliminate malnutrition in vulnerable groups of the population, and, in particular, a) serious protein-calorie malnutrition and anemia in children up to five years of age, and b) nutritional deficiencies in pregnant and nursing women.

In spite of a 90 percent rise in the consumer food price index between 1973 and 1975, measures to support these goals enabled the reduction of protein-calorie malnutrition in rural areas, and prevented deterioration in urban areas. This was accomplished by a shift from growing export crops (bananas) to foods for local consumption, the taxation of idle lands, land redistribution, higher wages, and reduced unemployment. An education program for community health aides reinforced the self-reliant theory of development, and may have had further impact upon nutritional status (Marchione, 1977).

Food Policy: The Chinese Example

The most important and awe-inspiring example of what can be done with coherent policy and political will is that of the People's Republic of China, which has managed to virtually eliminate serious malnutrition in a few decades. China has, by all accounts, solved its food problem. This solution has been brought about by two fundamental policy components — increasing food supplies through agricultural growth, and ensuring access to those food supplies by means of socialist distribution mechanisms (Timmer, 1976). Increase in production has been largely the result of Green Revolution, high-yielding strains of grain, coupled with labor-intensive rather than energy-intensive innovations, including double-cropping, major water control works, transportation facilities, and the utilization of large amounts of organic manure. Rural electrification has permitted the diffusion of manufacturing and repair capabilities into the countryside, while keeping motors simpler and cheaper to operate than those which use petroleum fuel. Significant diversification to include animal husbandry, fruit raising, beekeeping, food and fiber processing, and small-scale rural industries is now occurring. This is resulting in a transfer of workers from farm to factory, as in all industrializing countries, but the Chinese are unique in that the transfer involves shifts in occupation but not in location.

Access to food in China, as well as clothing, is insured by universal rationing of grain, cloth, and cooking oil. Families receive food grain ration coupons in quantities determined by the composition of the family, age of family members, and the occupation of the wage earners. Rations are large enough to provide some surplus, and "savings accounts" of grain can be established to draw upon at weddings and other feast occasions. No hoarding is needed. The poorest of the poor may have little access to other foods, but everyone has grain. As Timmer has put it, "China is still a very poor country. The wonder is not that many families cannot afford bicycles, transistor radios, or daily servings of meat, but that all can have three adequate, if starchy, meals each day. It would be no miracle for rich countries to solve their food problems, although the evidence is otherwise. China has done it while poor" (Timmer, 1976).

The Chinese example is obviously not exportable *in toto* to other nations. But it should be studied to determine which aspects may be adapted to other situations.

Perspective on a U.S. Role

To return to the National Academy of Sciences study team and the underlying assumption of its recommendations, the potential U.S. role in the solution of problems of hunger and malnutrition is complex. What the U.S. government is able to do about mobilizing U.S. nutrition research capability to assist the developing countries is related in part to what the U.S. government decides to do about its *own* nutrition problems. Thus, for example, urging by U.S. experts that developing countries adopt national nutrition policies and programs is likely to be regarded as somewhat anomalous in light of the fact that the U.S. government itself has never done so. Other countries may properly ask what the U.S. has done or intends to do about the nutrition problems of its own low-income populations, or what research evidence exists on the effectiveness of nutrition programs in the U.S.

To approach the task as one solely of helping to find answers for the developing countries would be viewed by some as another patronizing U.S. activity reflecting the assumption that the U.S. has all of the answers. This is clearly not the case in the field of nutrition. Indian scientists are ahead of their American counterparts in understanding the relationships between malnutrition and infection; Mexico, Guatemala, and Colombia lead the field in the area of nutrition and learning.

The research priorities outlined in the Academy study should be undertaken by U.S. scientists as part of an evolving international network of nutritional research. The international cooperation sought is not primarily governmental, but among scientific communities. The role of the U.S. government is to finance nutrition research and development where it can best be done. Country-specific problems can best be studied in the research institutes of those countries. Research and development that is not country-specific can be done anywhere. The contribution that the U.S. can

make most easily in this regard is to mobilize the energies and ingenuity of
U.S. and foreign scientists working in the United States. The supply of
qualified nutrition scientists is grossly inadequate, and the U.S. can also make
a significant contribution in training the needed individuals.

In summary, the solution of the world's food problems will only come
about through decreased population growth, rising incomes, accelerated
research in the U.S. and elsewhere, and a combination of policies and
programs, based on sufficient political will, to make the alleviation of hunger
and malnutrition a high-priority objective.

References

Adams, R.N.
  1974   Some observations on the inter-relations of development and nutrition
                programs. *Ecology of Food and Nutrition 3:* 85.

Austin, J.E.
  1975   Food and nutrition policies in a changing environment. *World Revue of
                Nutrition and Dietetics 25:* 108.

Berg, A.
  1973   *The Nutrition Factor: Its Role in National Development.* Brookings
                Institution, Washington, D.C.

Haas, J.D. and G.G. Harrison
  1977   *Annual Revue of Anthropology 6:* 69.

Holden, C.
  1977   Panel calls for global food and nutrition research drive. *Science
                197:* 140.

Marchione, T.J.
  1977   Food and nutrition in self-reliant national development: the impact on
                child nutrition of Jamaican government policy. *Medical Anthropology
                I,* 1:57.

National Academy of Sciences/National Research Council
  1977   *World Food and Nutrition Study,* Volumes I-V. National Academy of
                Sciences, Washington, D.C.

Reutlinger, S.
  1976   Nutrition Policy Research Priorities: A Perspective for the World Banks'
                Role. Unpublished manuscript.

Timmer, C.P.
  1976   *Food Research Institute Studies XV:* 1.

Timmer, C.P.
  n.d.   Access to Food: The Ultimate Determinant of Hunger. Unpublished
                manuscript.

World Food Conference
  1974   Proposals for Action: Section II, Policies and Programmes for
                Improving Nutrition. Rome: Unpublished working document, pp.
                137-162.

INDEX

[153]